Descriptive Catalogue of Australian Tradesmen's Tokens: Illustrated with Woodcuts, Also Some Account of the Early Silver Pieces and Gold Coinage of Australia

C W. Stainsfield

DESCRIPTIVE CATALOGUE

OF

AUSTRALIAN TRADESMEN'S TOKENS

ILLUSTRATED WITH WOODCUTS;

Also some account of the EARLY SILVER PIECES, and

GOLD COINAGE of AUSTRALIA.

BY

C. W. STAINSFIELD.

London:

C. W. STAINSFIELD,

Dealer in Ancient and Modern Coins, Medals and Tokens,

66, HOLBORN VIADUCT, E.C.

1883.

INTRODUCTION.

THE want of an authorized and efficient subsidiary coinage, has at various times had the effect of bringing into circulation large numbers of tokens issued by tradesmen and others.

In England between the years 1648 and 1672 an enormous issue of tradesmen's tokens took place, and Boyne in his valuable work arranges and describes nearly 9,500 varieties, and estimates that not less than 20,000 varieties were actually struck.

Towards the latter end of the eighteenth century, another large issue of copper tokens took place in England, and Boyne's remarks concerning the issue of the seventeenth century tokens, applies equally well to this issue of provincial coins or tokens, that "they "originated with a public necessity, but in the end became a "nuisance." The well known broad-edged penny, of which about 18 millions were issued, did away with the necessity; and an Act of Parliament, dated 27th June, 1817, finally prevented the issuing and circulating of copper tokens in England.

A great issue of tokens has taken place in the United States of America, and Canada has also found the necessity of supplying the wants of the people, some of the Canadian Bank tokens being of great beauty.

The Australian tokens, apart from supplying a want, at the time severely felt, were nevertheless a source of considerable profit to the issuer. Several of the tokens intended for circulation as pence, each weigh but the third of an ounce, and some few specimens barely that. This however, is an exception, as the average weight of the penny piece is a little over half an ounce. One token that circulated freely in the Colonies, issued by a Birmingham maker, boldly states upon it that " The Australian "Tokens are very profitable to export," and this advice was well acted upon; and the large issue of Australian tokens may therefore be said to have answered a three-fold purpose—utility, profit, and advertisement. This splendid opportunity was not lost sight of by Professor Holloway of Pill and Ointment notoriety, who thrust into circulation in our various Colonies immense numbers of pence and half-pence bearing his portrait.

Many of the tokens of this series were executed in England, and these are generally well made, and frequently bear pretty arrangements of Arms, Emblems, and Devices, typical of the country. Amongst them will be found some rather rough specimens of early Colonial workmanship. The greater part of the series, however, appear to have been made by Thomas Stokes of Melbourne, and this portion are all creditably engraved and neatly finished.

These tokens are very minutely described in German, in a valuable work published at Prague by Josef Neumann.* Volume three of this work describes 108 varieties, and 67 more specimens are described in the supplement published some few years later in the sixth volume; but by far the best work that has yet appeared is the catalogue prepared by Adolph Weyl of Berlin, of the Fourobert collection, sold by auction during the year 1878.

In this valuable work these tokens are described with an accuracy and minuteness that can only be met with in German catalogues; we English having an unfortunate manner of neglecting such coins and tokens as have no intrinsic value. No English catalogue having yet appeared, I am induced to think that no more favorable opportunity than the present will offer itself for forming a more complete collection of these tokens, and although I do not for a moment pretend that this catalogue is absolutely complete—the New Zealand tokens still being issued, and the collection having been formed in England—yet as far as Australia proper is concerned, where the issue of these tokens was suppressed in 1864, I believe the catalogue to be almost entire.

---

* " Beschreibung der bekanntesten Kupfer-münzen," von Josef Neumann, Prag, 1858-72. (This work is in six volumes, and describes 40,100 modern Copper Coins and Tokens of the whole world.)

I have found it impracticable to conform to any particular √
rule in describing these tokens, and have therefore, as far as
possible, *described them as they are intended to read.* In many
instances they are front and back simply advertisements, so that
it is immaterial which is described as the obverse, or which is
described as the reverse. In most instances the *obverse* will give
the name, trade, and address of the issuer. Arms, emblems, and
devices are consequently described as on the *reverse.*

The Australian tokens are taken first, and arranged in towns
alphabetically, the names of the issuers are also in alphabetical
order in each town. The New Zealand tokens follow, and are
treated in the same manner. A complete index of tradesmen's
names, &c., will be found at the end of the catalogue.

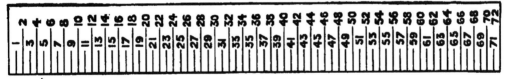

Scale according to American Standard of 1-16th of an inch.

SILVER AND GOLD COINS AND TOKENS.

English money has from the earliest period been the authorised currency in all the Australian Colonies, but the supply has at no time been equal to the demand. In the early days of New South Wales, the greater portion of the currency consisted of private notes issued by merchants, tradesman and publicans, many of which were for sums of six-pence, one shilling and upwards.

The first coin issued exclusively for the use of the Colony was in 1813.

No. 1. Rare.

A Charles the IIII. 1791 Spanish dollar with a piece stamped out of the centre 11-16ths of an inch in diameter.

Obv: FIVE SHILLINGS. Two sprigs of laurel each six leaves completing a circle. Countermarked around the inner edge.

Rev: NEW SOUTH WALES 1813, also countermarked around the inner edge.

No. 2. Rare.

Obv: A Crown in centre. NEW SOUTH WALES in half-circle above. 1813 beneath.

Rev: FIFTEEN | PENCE in two straight lines in centre.

This coin weighs 88 grains, and has a rough milling around the edge. It is formed of the piece stamped out of the dollar (No. 1), thus making the Spanish dollar represent six shillings and three-pence.

Silver coin was at this period so scarce, that in England Spanish dollars of Charles the IIII. were being re-struck for the Bank of England, who were paying them, and receiving them at the rate of five shillings and sixpence each.

Nos. 3 & 4.

The two following coins I have been unable to meet with, but after very careful consideration I have little doubt of their existence. Some collectors may have probably come across them, and being unable to classify them, have passed them by, and so ultimately have destined them to the melting-pot. They are mentioned in Mossman's little book, entitled "Our Australian "Colonies," and as it will be necessary to rely upon him for a description of them, I take the following from page 142 of his work :—

"From lack of specie, during the time of the war with "France, when gold was at a high premium in England, Spanish "dollars became a standard currency both in notes and metal, "and at one time the latter grew so scarce, that a piece was "struck out of the middle, about the size of a shilling, for which "sum it passed, and was called a 'dump,' while the mutilated "coin was called a 'ring dollar' as legal tender for four shillings, "both stamped with the King's head. This bastard money was "not plentiful, as the only source from whence it could be "obtained was at the commissariat, where the supplies to that "department were monopolized by four or five contractors."

They were issued for circulation in Tasmania.

Spanish dollars were countermarked with the King's head in England, between the years 1797 and 1803; but it is probable that the two coins in question circulated at about the same time as the two preceding coins of New South Wales, with which I have endeavoured to reconcile them; but the fact that they are distinctly stated to have been countermarked with the King's head, and again, that they were to pass for four shillings and one shilling respectively, renders it impossible to arrive at any conclusion other, than that they were distinct and separate coins.

No. 5. Tasmanian shilling, 1823. Very rare.

Obv: ONE | SHILLING | TOKEN in three lines in centre, SAW MILLS above, MACINTOSH AND DEGRAVES in three parts of a circle beneath.

Rev: A Kangaroo standing, TASMANIA in half-circle above, 1823 beneath.

This token is described from one in the collection of the British Museum.

No. 6.

Obv: GOVERNMENT ASSAY OFFICE ✱ ADELAIDE ✱ a crown, 1852 beneath, in centre of an inner circle with ornamental border.

Rev: WEIGHT. 5 DWT: 15 GRS: ✱ 22 CARATS ✱ — VALUE | ONE | POUND in three lines within an inner circle with ornamental border.

These tokens, which are well executed, weigh $12\frac{1}{2}$ grains more than the English sovereign, and are of the same fineness. They were issued by the South Australian Government on their own responsibility, to meet a pressing demand for gold coin caused by the influx of Victorian gold into the Colony, and consequent large purchases of Crown lands, the price of which was payable only in gold. They circulated freely until the introduction of the Sydney sovereign in 1855.

No. 7. Gold. Size 22. Very rare.

Obv: A Kangaroo, 1853 beneath. PORT PHILLIP — AUS- TRALIA inscribed in sunken letters on broad raised rim.

Rev: A large 2. The words TWO OUNCES in sunken letters on the figure. PURE AUSTRALIAN GOLD — TWO OUNCES inscribed in sunken letters on a broad-raised rim. Edges milled.

No. 8. Gold. Size $17\frac{1}{2}$. Very rare.

Obv: Same as No. 7.

Rev: Same as reverse of No. 7, excepting that the figure in centre is 1, and the words ONE OUNCE are in sunken letters on the figure.

No. 9. Gold. Size 14. Very rare.

Obv: Same as No. 7.

Rev: Same as No. 7, excepting that the figures ($\frac{1}{2}$) in centre are quite plain.

No. 10. Gold. Size 12. Very rare.

Obv: Same as No. 7.

Rev: Same as No. 7, excepting that the figures ($\frac{1}{4}$) in centre are quite plain.

These four tokens are in the British Museum. There are also two specimens in the United States National Mint Collection at Philadelphia, viz. the 2-oz. piece and the $\frac{1}{2}$-oz. piece. The larger of these two pieces is engraved in Snowden's Ancient and Modern Coins.* It is doubtful whether these pieces were ever intended for circulation, as they appear to have been struck more as a memento of the great gold discoveries.

No. 11.

Obv: Head of Queen Victoria in centre. VICTORIA in indented letters on broad raised rim above. AUSTRALIA in sunken letters on broad raised rim beneath the head, the broad rim grained.

Rev: Large 6 with grained surface in centre. SIXPENCE in indented letters on broad raised rim, in half-circle above the 6.

This six-pence from the cabinet of Mr. J. G. Goll was sold by Messrs. Sotheby, Wilkinson & Hodge, April 25th, 1882, for £3 10s. 0d. It was described in the catalogue as an "Australian "Six-pence; a rare gem." I have never seen any other specimen, and should take it to be a pattern for a token.

No. 12. (Silver Three-pence.)

Obv: A tree. Kangaroo to left. Emu to right. HOGARTH ERICHSEN & Co JEWELLERS SYDNEY.

Rev: Two Oak branches tied together in the form of a wreath. In centre a large 3, and date 1858 (18 to left of figure, 58 to right).

No. 13. (Silver Three-pence.)

Obv: A specie of Gum Plant in centre. Kangaroo to right. Emu to left. HOGARTH ERICHSEN & CO in three parts of a circle around the Kangaroo and Emu. SYDNEY in straight line beneath.

Rev: Same as No. 12.

* "A description of Ancient and Modern Coins, in the Cabinet Collection "at the Mint of the United States. Prepared and arranged under the direc- "tion of James Ross Snowden." Philadelphia, 1860.

No. 14. (Silver Three-pence.)

Obv: A Tree. Kangaroo to left. Emu to right. PAYABLE AT HOGARTH ERICHSEN & Co—SYDNEY beneath.

Rev: Same as No. 12.

No. 15. (Silver Threepence.)

Obv: A Yellow Gum Plant. Kangaroo to left. Emu to right. REMEMBRANCE—OF AUSTRALIA.

Rev: A large 3 in centre, surrounded by two olive branches tied together in the form of a wreath. HOGARTH & ERICHSEN —SYDNEY between the edge of coin and wreath. 1860 in minute figures above the word Sydney.

No. 16. (One Sovereign.)

Obv: VICTORIA D: G: BRITANNIAR: REGINA F: D: Head of Queen Victoria to left, undraped, round the head two plain bands, hair parted on forehead and carried over the ear. The whole gathered together at the back of the head in the form of a knot. 1855 beneath.

Rev: Two Olive branches forming a wreath tied together with a ribbon. AUSTRALIA surmounted by a crown, in centre. SYDNEY MINT above the wreath. ONE SOVEREIGN beneath.

No. 17. (Half-Sovereign.)

Similar to preceding. HALF SOVEREIGN beneath the wreath, on reverse.

Patterns for the Sovereign and Half-sovereign of this design were prepared in 1853, and specimens of the two coins are in the Mint Museum and in the British Museum. No actual issue, however, took place until 1855.

Sovereigns and Half-sovereigns of this design were also issued during the following year (1856).

No. 18. (Sovereign.)

Obv: VICTORIA D: G: BRITANNIAR: REG: F: D: Head of Queen Victoria to the left, undraped, laurel wreath around the head, hair plaited; one plait carried under the ear, and the whole gathered together at the back of the head in a knot. 1857 beneath.

Rev: Same as No. 16.

No. 19. (Half-sovereign.)

Similar to preceding. HALF SOVEREIGN beneath the wreath, on reverse.

A pattern for the half-sovereign of this design was prepared in 1856, and a very beautiful specimen with plain edge, bearing that date, was formerly in the possession of the late Mr. Bergne, and afterwards in the cabinet of Mr. J. H. Young of Lee. By a singular mistake, it is incorrectly described in both the sale catalogues of these gentlemen's coins. In Mr. Bergne's sale it is described as a proof "half-sovereign of 1870," and in Mr. Young's as "a proof half-sovereign 1856 *usual type.*" This coin, with a proof sovereign of 1870, brought at the latter gentleman's sale in April, 1881, the rather high price of £5.

The Sydney branch of the Royal Mint was opened on the 14th of May, 1855, exclusively for the coinage of gold into Sovereigns and Half Sovereigns. The dies for the coins having been engraved at the Royal Mint in London.

The following table will show the number of coins issued between 1855 and 1870 :—

DATE.		Type described in catalogue as	Number of Coins.	VALUE.
1855-6	Sovereigns	No. 16	1,488,000	1,488,000
do.	Hlf. Sovereigns	No. 17	499,100	249,500
1857 to 1870	Sovereigns	No. 18	24,484,500	24,484,500
do.	Hlf. Sovereigns	No. 19	2,760,000	1,880,000
				£27,547,000

No Half Sovereigns were struck in the years 1862, 1864, 1866, 1868 and 1870.

The following table taken from the Report of the Deputy-Master of the Sydney Branch of the Royal Mint, shows year by year the number of coins and their value, from the date of the establishment of the Mint in 1855 to the year 1870, when the distinct type for Australia was discontinued.

Date.	Sovereigns.	Number of Half Sovereigns.	Total Value.
1855	502,000	21,000	512,500
1856	981,000	478,000	1,220,000
1857	499,000	537,000	767,500
1858	1,101,500	483,000	1,843,000
1859	1,050,500	341,000	1,221,000
1860	1,578,500	156,000	1,651,500
1861	1,626,000	186,500	1,719,250
1862	2,477,500	———	2,477,500
1863	1,255,500	558,500	1,584,750
1864	2,698,500	———	2,698,500
1865	2,130,500	282,000	2,271,500
1866	2,911,000	———	2,911,000
1867	2,370,000	62,000	2,401,000
1868	2,819,000	———	2,819,000
1869	1,202,000	154,000	1,279,000
1870	1,220,000	———	1,220,000
	£25,917,500	£3,259,000	£27,547,000

There is no doubt that when the Sydney Mint was established, it was intended that the coins struck at this Mint should supply the demand for gold coin in the Australian colonies only, and it was no part of the scheme that England should draw these coins to supplement her gold currency. Still immense numbers of these Sovereigns found their way to England, and the money changers for a time reaped a considerable benefit from them, charging as they did, sixpence and more for exchange on each coin, causing considerable dissatisfaction. This state of things was, however, remedied by a proclamation, dated February 6th, 1867, declaring all Australian Sovereigns and their halves, to be current coin of the realm.

A second Australian branch of the Royal Mint commenced operations in Melbourne during the month of May, 1871, for the coinage of gold, and all coins issued from this Mint as well as the Sydney Mint, after the end of the year 1870 are identical with the English Sovereign and its half. A minute mint' mark, S for Sydney, and M for Melbourne, only distinguishing the Australian gold from that coined at the Royal Mint. It is placed immediately over the rose at the foot of the design of those sovereigns, having for a *reverse* arms in a plain shield crowned and encircled with a laurel wreath. And beneath the bust on the *obverse* of those sovereigns struck since 1871 that have for the reverse St. George armed, sitting on horseback attacking the Dragon.

The immense value of the two Australian branch Mints may be easily seen from the fact that our own Mint during the year 1881 struck no gold coins whatever, whilst the two Australian Mints issued no less a sum than £3,736,800. And no doubt this will be greatly exceeded when the returns come in for 1882, owing to the demand for gold, and the re-construction of the Royal Mint; which caused it to be absolutely closed for the greater part of the year.

TRADESMEN'S COPPER TOKENS.

Adelaide (South Australia).

No. 20. Penny. Size 21. Common.

Obv: CROCKER | & | HAMILTON | ADELAIDE | PORT ADELAIDE displayed in five lines.

Rev: CROKER | & | HAMILTON in three lines in centre. DRAPERS in half circle above. CLOTHIERS &c., in half circle beneath.

No. 21. Halfpenny. Size 17½. Common.

Obv: CROCKER AND HAMILTON 1857 around the token between the dotted edge and inner circle. DRAPERS | SILK MERCERS | AND | CLOTHIERS in four lines within the circle in centre.

Rev: ADELAIDE, PORT ADELAIDE. AND BURRA BURRA. around the token between the dotted edge and inner circle. A view of the Shop within the circle in centre. REGENT HOUSE above the door. TAILORS on window plate to left. DRAPERS on window plate to right.

No. 22. Penny. Size 21. Common.

Obv: HARROLD BROTHERS | WHOLESALE | & | RE-TAIL | IRONMONGERS | HINDLEY St. | ADELAIDE displayed in seven lines.

Rev: Female seated on a bale, eyes bandaged; holding scales in right hand and horn of plenty (cornucopia) in left, out of which is issuing fruits and flowers. Cask at back. Water and ship in the distance. AUSTRALIA in half circle above. 1858 beneath.

No. 23. Penny. Size 21. Common.

Obv: JOHN HOWELL | BOOKSELLER | RUNDLE St. | ADELAIDE displayed in four lines.

Rev : A Bird holding an olive branch in its mouth (The Liver,—The Crest, on the Arms of the City of Liverpool, England) LIVERPOOL in half circle above. CHEAP BOOK DEPOT in half circle beneath.

No. 24. Penny. Size 21. Common.

Obv : JOHN HOWELL | BOOKSELLER | HINDLEY St. | ADELAIDE displayed in four lines.

Rev : Same as reverse of preceding (No. 23.)

No. 25. Penny. Size 21. Common.

Obv : JOHN MARTIN | GROCER | AND | TEA DEALER | 29 | RUNDLE STREET | ADELAIDE displayed in seven lines.

Rev : Female standing facing left, eyes bandaged ; holding scales in right hand, and horn of plenty in left, out of which is issuing fruits and flowers. Water and ship in the distance. AUSTRALIA in half circle above the figure.

No. 26. Penny. Size 21. Common.

Obv : MARTIN & SACH in half circle. IRONMONGERS in straight line in centre. ADELAIDE in half circle beneath.

Rev : Same as reverse of preceding (No. 25.)

No. 27. Penny. Size 21. Common.

Obv : WILLIAM MORGAN | WHOLESALE | & | RETAIL | GROCER | HINDLEY STREET | ADELAIDE—displayed in seven lines.

Rev : Same as reverse of No. 22.

No. 28. Penny. Size 21. Common.

Obv : ALFRED TAYLOR | DRAPER | AND | CLOTHIER | ADELAIDE | 31 RUNDLE STREET displayed in six lines.

Rev : Same as reverse of No. 25.

Ballarat (Victoria).

The name of the town on this token is spelt with two a's (Ballaarat). It was common to find it spelt this way in the early days of the Colony, being more in accordance with the name as pronounced by the natives, but the generally accepted way of spelling the word is now Ballarat.

No. 29. Penny. Size 21. Common.

Obv: J. R. GRUNDY . MERCHANT, BALLAARAT . 1861. A tobacco plant in flower in centre. TOBACCO beneath the plant.

Rev: Australian Arms in centre. INDUSTRIA ET FIDES OMNIA VINCENT (Industry and Faith overcomes all things.) In three parts of a circle around the upper portion of Arms. VICTORIA beneath.

The "Australian Arms" on this token may be thus described. A Shield supported on the right by a Kangaroo, and on the left by an Emu. The Shield is quartered 1st, a Golden Fleece. 2nd, a Ship. 3rd, an Ox. 4th, an Anchor. Crest, a rising Sun with rays. Motto, Advance Australia (on scroll). These "Arms" appear on the reverse of many of the tokens throughout the series, and in a great number of instances vary very considerably. The specimen, No. 33, gives the Arms as supported on the *right* by the Emu and on the *left* by the Kangaroo, and the quartering of the Shield is entirely different; indeed, the quartering of the Shield varies in almost every instance, such emblems as a Golden Fleece, a Ship, an Ox, an Anchor, a Wheatsheaf, a Pick and Shovel, &c., being so placed as to suit the taste or caprice of the issuer or engraver, for, as a matter of fact, *no Arms have ever been granted to Australia*, and it therefore becomes a remarkable feature that the general design has been so faithfully adhered to.

No. 30. Penny. Size 21. Scarce.

Obv: J. R. GRUNDY MERCHANT BALLARAT . 1861 . A sprig of the tobacco plant in flower, in centre.

Rev: INDUSTRIA ET FIDES OMNIA VINCET . VICTORIA on a raised rim. Female standing facing left, holding scales in right hand and horn of plenty in left, out of which is issuing fruits and flowers. Water and Ship in the distance—in centre, within a dotted circle.

No. 31. Penny. Size 21. Scarce.

Obv: DAVID JONES | IMPORTER | BALLAARAT | ESTAB: 1853 in four lines in centre. CRITERION DRAPERY ESTABLISHMENT ✱ WHOLESALE AND RETAIL ✱ around the token.

Rev: CRITERION HOUSE | STURT St. | BALLAARAT 1862 | DAVID JONES PROPRIETOR. A view of Criterion House in centre.

No. 32. Penny. Size 21. Scarce.

Obv: SOUTHWARD | & | SUMPTON | BALLARAT displayed in four lines within a circle in centre. WHOLESALE GROCERS ✱ WINE & SPIRIT MERCHANTS ✱ around the token between the circle and the dotted edge.

Rev: SOUTHWARD & SUMPTON BALLARAT — Australian Arms in centre. ADVANCE BALLARAT on scroll (the Arms are quartered with a Ship, a Golden Fleece, a Spade and Pick crossed, and a Wheatsheaf.)

B

No. 33. Penny. Size 21. Scarce.

Obv: J. TAYLOR | RED HOUSE | CORNER OF | DANNA & RAGLAN | STREETS | BALLARAT displayed in six lines within a circle in centre. BREAD AND BISCUIT BAKER FAMILY GROCER: around the token, between the dotted edge and circle.

Rev: Australian Arms ADVANCE VICTORIA on scroll at foot. In the shield are double lines forming a cross, a star in centre, and four other stars, one at each extremity. In the four corners of the Shield, a Ship, a Golden Fleece, an Anchor and a Wheatsheaf. VICTORIA 1862 above. T STOKES MAKER | 100 COLLINS ST. EAST MELBOURNE in a half circle beneath the Arms.

No. 34. Penny. Size 21. Scarce.

Obv: Same as No. 33.

Rev: ADVANCE AUSTRALIA in half circle above. A Wheatsheaf in centre. 1862 beneath.

No. 35. Penny. Size 21. Scarce.

Obv: Same as No. 33.

Rev: VICTORIA 1862: IN VINO VERITAS: (in wine is truth). A branch of a vine with grapes and leaves. T. STOKES-MAKER MEL within a circle in centre.

This token is not in my possession, but is described in Adolph Weyls' catalogue of the Fonrobert collection.

No. 36. Penny. Size 21. Scarce.

Obv: W. R. WATSON & CO. in straight line across the centre. WINE & SPIRIT MERCHANTS | TOWN HALL HOTEL ARMSTRONG ST. BALLARAT arranged in two circular lines around the token.

Rev: Same as No. 35.

No. 37. Penny. Size 21. Scarce.

Obv : Same as No. 36.

Rev : Same as No. 35, excepting that the name T. STOKES MAKER MEL is larger, and the number and disposition of leaves on the vine branch vary.

(For the several varieties of this reverse see No. 170 and upwards, T. Stokes.)

Bathurst (New South Wales.)

No. 38. Penny. Size 21. Scarce.

Obv : COLLINS | & CO. within a circle in centre. CHEAP CLOTHING BAZAAR : BATHURST : around the token between the dotted edge and circle.

Rev : A Kangaroo and Emu facing. NEW SOUTH WALES in half circle above. 1864 beneath. T. STOKES beneath the Emu. MELBOURNE beneath the Kangaroo.

Bendigo (Victoria.)

This town is now named Sandhurst. It was a celebrated and early diggings, and was called Bendigo, after the pugilist of that name.

No. 39. Penny. Size 21. Scarce.

Obv : HODGSON BROs. | SAILORS | GULLY | & | CALE-FORNIA | GULLY | BENDIGO displayed in seven lines within a circle in centre. WHOLESALE & RETAIL GROCERS & PRODUCE MERCHANTS : around the token between the circle and the dotted edge.

Rev: An Emu. Sun rays at back. ADVANCE VICTORIA on scroll at foot of Emu. VICTORIA 1862 above. T. STOKES MAKER. | 100 COLLINS ST. EAST MELBOURNE in two lines at foot.

Brisbane (Queensland.)

No. 40. Penny. Size 21. Common.

Obv: BROOKES in straight line in centre. IRONMONGERS in half circle above. BRISBANE in half circle beneath.

Rev: Same as obverse.

No. 41. Penny. Size 22. Scarce.

The design of this token is the same as No. 40, excepting that the letters in the words IRONMONGERS and BRISBANE are ornamental instead of plain.

No. 42. Penny. Size 21. Common.

Obv: W. & B. BROOKES | IRONMONGERS | BRISBANE in three lines.

Rev: Australian Arms. QUEENSLAND above. 1863 beneath. The quartering of the Arms are similar to those shown on No. 29.

No. 43. Penny. Size 21. Scarce.

Obv: J. W. BUXTON in straight lines across centre. STATIONERY in half circle above. STORES in half circle beneath.

Rev: LADIES WAREHOUSE in half circle above. BRISBANE straight line in centre. : QUEENSLAND : in half circle beneath.

No. 44. Penny. Size 20½. Common.

Obv: ONE | PENNY in two straight lines in centre. LARCOMBE & COMPy. in half circle above. ✱ BRISBANE ✱ beneath.

Rev: LARCOMBE | & | COMPy. in three lines in centre. FURNISHING DRAPERS TAILORS &c. ✱ around the token.

No. 45. Penny. Size 20½.

Obv: Same as reverse of No. 44.

Rev: Same as reverse of No. 47. This is most probably a mule.

No. 46. Penny. Size 21. Common.

Obv: J. SAWYER | WHOLESALE | & RETAIL | TO-BACCONIST | BRISBANE displayed in five lines.

Rev: Australian Arms. QUEENSLAND above. 1864 beneath. The Arms are quartered with a Golden Fleece, an Anchor, a Ship and a Wheatsheaf. ADVANCE AUSTRALIA on scroll.

No. 47. Penny. Size 21. Common.

Obv: STEWART & HEMMANT ✳ DRAPERS ✳ — ONE | PENNY | in two lines in centre.

Rev: CRITERION. BRISBANE & ROCKHAMPTON. An Emu in centre. W. J. TAYLOR . LONDON in minute letters under the Emu.

No. 48. Penny. Size 19. Scarce.

Obv: STEWART & HEMMANT in half circle above. CRITERION straight line in centre. BRISBANE beneath.

Rev: DRAPERS in straight line across centre. WHOLE-SALE in half circle above. RETAIL in half circle beneath.

Campbell Town (Tasmania.)

No. 49. Penny. Size 21. Scarce.

Obv: JOSEPH BRICKHILL in half circle above. DRAPER | AND | GENERAL | IMPORTER in four straight lines in centre. CAMPBELL TOWN in half circle beneath.

Rev: ONE PENNY TOKEN in half circle above. AD-VANCE | TASMANIA | 1856 in three straight 'lines in centre. COMMERCIAL HOUSE in half circle beneath.

Castlemaine (Victoria.)

No. 50. Penny. Size 21. Common.

Obv: T. BUTTERWORTH & Co. in half circle above. 1 | FOREST | STREET in three lines in centre. CASTLE-MAINE beneath.

Rev: WHOLESALE & RETAIL GROCERS & DRAPERS ✳ around the token. WINE | & | SPIRIT | MERCHANTS in four straight lines in centre.

No. 51. Penny. Size 21. Common.

Same as No. 50, excepting that the letters on the obverse are bolder, and the figure 1, is larger.

No. 52. Penny. Size 21. Common.

Obv: Same as No. 50.

Rev: Female seated on a bale. Eyes bandaged; holding Scales in right hand, and horn of plenty in left, out of which is issuing fruits and flowers. Cask at back. Water and Ship in the distance. 1859 beneath.

No. 53. Penny. Size 21. Scarce.

Obv: R. CALDER | BARKER ST. | CASTLEMAINE displayed in three lines within a circle in centre. WINE SPIRIT & GENERAL PROVISION MERCHANT: 1862: around the token, between the dotted edge and inner circle.

Rev: Same as No. 33.

No. 54. Penny. Size 21. Scarce.

Obv: W. FROOMES | MARKET SQᴿ. | CASTLEMAINE displayed in three lines within a circle in centre. FAMILY DRAPER CLOTHIER & OUTFITTER: around the token between the dotted edge and inner circle.

Rev: Same as No. 33.

No. 55. Penny. Size 21. Common.

Obv: MURRAY | AND | CHRISTIE | CASTLEMAINE displayed in four lines.

Rev: GROCERS | IRONMONGERS | CHINA & GLASS | WARE | MERCHANTS in five straight lines.

No. 56. Penny. Size 21. Scarce.

Obv: Same as reverse of No. 55.

Rev: Same as 33.

This token is a "mule," and was probably issued by Thomas Stokes, the maker. I have met with several specimens, all of which have been in circulation.

No. 57. Penny. Size 21. Common.

Obv: G. RYLAND | DRAPER | AND | CLOTHIER | MARKET SQᴿᴱ· | CASTLEMAINE displayed in six lines.

Rev: Same as No. 33.

Deloraine (Tasmania.)

No. 58. Penny. Size 21. Scarce.

Obv: SAMUEL HENRY between two straight lines across the centre. DELORAINE in half circle above, beneath which is a dotted half circle. EMPORIUM in half circle beneath the name, and dotted half circle above.

Rev: A Kangaroo and Emu facing. TASMANIA in half circle above. 1857 beneath.

Eagle Hawk (Victoria.)

No. 59. Penny. Size 21. Scarce.

Obv: R. GRIEVE in straight line in centre. EAGLE above. HAWK beneath. The whole within a circle. WHOLE-SALE & RETAIL GROCER: around the token between the dotted edge and inner circle.

Rev: Same as No. 33.

No. 60. Penny. Size 21. Scarce.

Obv: J. W. & G. WILLIAMS | GROCERS | IRON-MONGERS | & | DRAPERS | EAGLE HAWK displayed in six lines.

Rev: GOLD OFFICE | WINE, SPIRIT | & | COLONIAL | PRODUCE | MERCHANTS | EAGLE HAWK displayed in seven lines.

Freemantle (Western Australia.)

No. 61. Penny. Size 19. Scarce.

Obv: ALFRED DAVIES in half circle. PAWNBROKER in straight line in centre. HIGH S$^{T.}$ FREMANTLE in half circle beneath.

Rev: A Swan swimming. WESTERN AUSTRALIA in half circle above. 1865 beneath.

This is the only Western Australian token that I have met with. The Swan is emblematical of the former name of the settlement—Swan River.

Geelong (Victoria.)

No. 62. Penny. Size 21. Very common.

Obv: R. PARKER | IRONMONGER in two lines in centre. MOORABOOL STREET in half circle above. GEE-LONG in half circle beneath.

Rev: Female standing facing left, eyes bandaged; holding scales in right hand, and cornucopia in left, out of which is issuing fruits and flowers. Water and ship in the distance. AUSTRALIA in half circle above the figure (same as reverse of No. 25.)

No. 63. Penny. Size 21. Common.

Obv: Same as No. 62, excepting that the letters are a trifle larger, especially noticeable in the name R. PARKER.

Rev: Same as No. 62.

No. 64. Penny. Size 21. Common.

Obv: Same as No. 62, excepting that there are two dots (:) between the initial and the name R : PARKER, and a dot after the word IRONMONGER.

Rev: Same as No. 62.

No. 65. Penny. Size 21. Scarce.

Obv: Same as No. 64, excepting that the tail of the R's in the name R : PARKER are slightly curled up, and the word GEELONG is larger.

Rev: Same as No. 62.

I have only described four varieties of this token. Adolph Weyl, in his catalogue of the Fonrobert collection, describes seven, varying slightly in the disposition of the letters, both on the obverse and reverse. I have examined and compared many specimens of this issue, which was extremely large, and find that possibly not less than a dozen dies were used in the manufacture of the obverse alone.

Goulburn (New South Wales).

No. 66. Penny. Size 21. Scarce.

Obv : DAVIES, ALEXANDER & C⁰. GOULBURN.— A Golden Fleece within a dotted circle in centre.

Rev : AUSTRALIAN STORES | GOULBURN Australian Arms within a dotted circle in centre. ESTABLISHED above. 1837 beneath the Arms. The Arms are quartered with a Golden Fleece, a Ship, an Ox and an Anchor. ADVANCE AUSTRALIA on scroll.

Hobart Town (Tasmania.)

No. 67. Penny. Size 21. Common.

Obv : LEWIS ABRAHAMS | DRAPER | LIVERPOOL STREET | HOBART TOWN displayed in four lines.

Rev : A Kangaroo and Emu facing. (Kangaroo to right, Emu to left.) TASMANIA in half circle above. 1855 beneath.

No. 68. Halfpenny. Size 17½. Common.

Obverse and reverse same as preceding.

No. 69. Penny. Size 19. Scarce.

Obv : J. G. FLEMING. GROCER & TEA DEALER around the token between the dotted edge and inner circle. An ornamental wreath, within the circle in centre.

Rev : SUGAR LOAF . HOBART TOWN . 1874 around the token between the dotted edge and inner circle. A Sugar Loaf, with letter F upon it, within the circle in centre.

This token is in the British Museum collection.

No. 70. Penny. Size 21. Common.

Obv : I . FRIEDMAN in half circle. PAWNBROKER in straight line across centre. ARGYLE STREET in half circle beneath.

Rev : Female seated on a bale. Cask at back; holding scales in right hand, and horn of plenty in left, out of which is issuing fruits and flowers. Water and Ship in the distance. TASMANIA in half circle above. 1857 beneath.

No. 71. Halfpenny. Size 17. Common.

Obverse and reverse same as preceding. (The name of the town is omitted on these two tokens, Nos. 70 and 71.)

No. 72. Penny. Size 21. Common.

Obv: OIL & COLOR STORES in half circle above. O.H | HEDBERG in two straight lines in centre. * ARGYLE ST. HOBART TON * in half circle beneath.

Rev: * O.H.HEDBERG * SWEDISH HOUSE HOBART TON around the token. ONE | PENNY in two straight lines in centre.

No. 73. Halfpenny. Size 17½. Common.

Obv: Same as No. 72.

Rev: Same as No. 72, excepting that HALF | PENNY is in two lines in centre.

The following four tokens are "mules." They are in the finest condition, not having been in circulation. They appear to have been struck with a total disregard to the geography of the country; an obverse of the colony of Tasmania, to a reverse of the colony of Victoria; and again, an obverse of Tasmania, to a reverse of New Zealand. The figure on the reverse of No. 75 is beautifully executed, and is apparently a pattern, as I have never met with any specimen of the design amongst the tokens that have been in circulation.

No. 74. Penny. Size 21.

Obv: Same as No. 70.

Rev: Female seated on a bale, eyes bandaged; holding scales in right hand, and horn of plenty in left, out of which is issuing fruits and flowers. Cask at back. Water and Ship in the distance. MELBOURNE VICTORIA above the figure. 1860 beneath.

No. 75. Penny. Size 21.

Obv: Same as reverse of No. 70.

Rev: A female seated on a rock surrrounded by the sea. Ship in the distance. Olive branch in right hand. Wand in left.

AUSTRALIA above the figure. (W.J.TAYLOR—LONDON) at foot of design.

No. 76. Half-penny. Size 17½.

Obv: Same as reverse of No. 73.

Rev: Same as reverse of No. 102. (SIC VOS NON VOBIS VELLERA FERTIS OVES ✳ A golden fleece in centre.)

No. 77. Halfpenny. Size 17½.

Obv: Same as obverse of No. 73.

Rev: LIPMAN LEVY | IMPORTER | AND | MANU-FACTURER | OF BOOTS | & SHOES | WELLINGTON. NEW ZEALAND displayed in seven lines.

No. 78. Penny. Milled edge. Size 21. Scarce.

Obv: - R. HENRY - | WHOLESALE | AND RETAIL | IRONMONGER | 94 LIVERPOOL Sᵀ HOBART TOWN displayed in five lines.

Rev: ONE PENNY TOKEN PAYABLE ON DEMAND AT R. HENRY'S. In centre three saws crossed, and surrounded by spade, rake, scythe, sickle, fork, and other implements (12 in all).

No. 79. Penny. Size 21. Scarce.

Obv: G . HUTTON IRONMONGER . HOBART TOWN. A saw and sickle in centre.

Rev: Kangaroo and Emu facing, occupying the whole of the field.

No. 80. Halfpenny. Size 17½. Scarce.

Obv: and Rev: same as No. 79.

No. 81. Penny. Size 21. Common.

Obv: WILLIAM ANDREW JARVEY | PAWNBROKER | AND GENERAL | CLOTHIER | HOBART TOWN displayed in five lines.

Rev: ONE PENNY TOKEN PAYABLE AT W. A. JARVEY'S MURRAY STREET. Three balls suspended by chain from a staff in centre.

No. 82. Penny. Size 21. Common.

Obv: Same as No. 81.

Rev: Same as No. 81, excepting that the three balls are smaller, and suspended from a bracket. The balls are fixed by ornamental rods, and not hanging by chains as in the previous token.

No. 83. Penny. Size 21. Common.

Obv: H. LIPSCOMBE. MURRAY STREET. HOBART TOWN. ✱ SEEDSMAN & SALESMAN ✱ In centre an assortment of fruits and flowers.

Rev: SHIPPING SUPPLIED WITH ALL KINDS OF COLONIAL PRODUCE ✱ —ONE PENNY | TOKEN in two lines in centre.

No. 84. Penny. Size 21. Scarce.

Obv: H. J. MARSH & BROTHER | IRONMONGERS | | MURRY AND | COLLINS S^T· | HOBART TOWN displayed in five lines.

Rev: Within a double circle in centre, a chaff cutter's knife, a scythe head, and another implement. A spade and fork crossed beneath the circle. PAYABLE AT above. ONE SHILLING FOR 12 PENNY TOKENS. H. J. MARSH & BROTHER. around the token.

No. 85. Penny. Size 21. Scarce.

Obv: Same as obverse of No. 84, excepting the word MURRAY in the centre line, which is now spelt with an A.

Rev: A scythe head, two other knives or implements, and a spade and fork crossed. PAYABLE AT above the scythe head. —ONE SHILLING FOR 12 PENNY TOKENS. H.J.MARSH & BROTHER around the token.

No. 86. Halfpenny. Size 17. Scarce.

Obv: H. J. MARSH & BROTHER HOBART TOWN— IRONMONGERS in straight line in centre.

Rev: A steamer and water. HALFPENNY TOKEN above. TO FACILITATE TRADE beneath.

No. 87. Penny. Size 21. Very common.

Obv: R. ANDREW MATHER. | FAMILY | DRAPER | &c. | HOBART TOWN. displayed in five lines.

Rev: Female standing facing left, eyes bandaged, holding scales in right hand, and horn of plenty in left, out of which is issuing fruits and flowers. Water and Ship in the distance. TASMANIA above the figure.

No. 88. Penny. Size 21. Common.

Obv: JOSEPH MOIR | WHOLESALE | AND | RETAIL | IRONMONGERY | ESTABLISHMENT | 1850 | HOBART TOWN displayed in eight lines.

Rev: ONE | PENNY TOKEN | PAYABLE | ON DEMAND | HERE in five straight lines in centre. ECONOMY HOUSE in half circle above. MURRY STREET beneath.

No. 89. Penny. Size 21. Rare.

Obv: LIVERPOOL TEA WAREHOUSE * HOBARTON* ——A. NICHOLAS | 30 | Liverpool St. in three lines in centre.

Rev: The Arms of Liverpool, England, occupying the whole of the field.

This token is most probably of Colonial Workmanship, and one of the earliest specimens of the series.

No. 90. Penny. Size 21. Scarce.

Obv: ALFRED NICHOLAS | LIVERPOOL | TEA WARE-HOUSE | LIVERPOOL S^{T.} | HOBART TOWN displayed in five lines.

Rev: Britannia seated, holding olive branch in right hand. Trident over left shoulder. Shield at side. BRITANNIA in half circle above.

No. 91. Halfpenny. Size 17. Scarce.

Obv: and Rev: same as No. 90.

No. 92. Penny. Size 21. Common.

Obv: R. S. WATERHOUSE | DRAPERY | ESTABLISH-MENT | HOBART TOWN | ONE PENNY | TOKEN | MANCHESTER HOUSE displayed in seven lines.

Rev: A baby jumping by the aid of an apparatus known as a "baby jumper." BABY LINEN to left. WAREHOUSE to right. FOR READY MONEY THE SPIRIT OF TRADE around the token.

No. 93. Halfpenny. Size 17. Common.

Obv: R.S.WATERHOUSE | DRAPERY | ESTABLISH-MENT | HALFPENNY | TOKEN | MANCHESTER HOUSE displayed in six lines.

Rev: Same as reverse of No. 92.

No. 94. Penny. Size 21. Common.

Obv: W.D.WOOD | WINE | & | SPIRIT | MERCHANT in five lines in centre. MONTPELIER RETREAT. in half circle above. HOBART TOWN in half circle beneath.

Rev: A view of the Montpelier Retreat Inn. HOBART TOWN in half circle above. 1855 beneath.

No. 95. Penny. Size 21. Common.

Obv: ONE PENNY TOKEN | PAYABLE | ON DEMAND HERE | MONTPELLIER RETREAT | INN, | HOBART TOWN. | W.D. WOOD displayed in seven lines.

Rev: A view of the Inn, varying from the preceding by having two trees and a flagstaff at back. MONTPELLIER RETREAT INN in half circle above. W.D. WOOD beneath.

No. 96. Halfpenny. Size 17½. Common.

Obv: Same as No. 95, excepting that the first line reads ONE HALFPENNY TOKEN.

Rev: Same as reverse of No. 95.

Ipswich (Queensland.)

No. 97. Penny. Size 21. Common.

Obv: T.H.JONES | & Cº | IPSWICH | QUEENSLAND | AUSTRALIA in five lines in centre within a circle. IRON-MONGERS & GENERAL IMPORTERS around the token between the dotted edge and inner circle.

Rev: Same as No. 25.

No. 98. Penny. Size 19. Common.

Obv: JOHN PETTIGREW | & Cº | IPSWICH in three

lines in centre. WHOLESALE AND RETAIL GENERAL MERCHANTS around the token.

Rev: Australian Arms. QUEENSLAND above. 1865 beneath.

The arms are quartered with a golden fleece, a ship, an ox, and an anchor. ADVANCE AUSTRALIA on scroll.

No. 99. Halfpenny. Size 16. Common.

Same as No. 96.

These two tokens are bronze, and of the same size and weight as the English bronze coinage.

Jamberoo (New South Wales.)

No. 100. Penny. Size 21. Scarce. Rare, when fine.

Obv: WILLIAM ALLEN. JAMBEROO. In centre a floral device displaying the rose, thistle and shamrock. GENERAL STORES in circular form around the device.

Rev: Australian Arms. ADVANCE AUSTRALIA above. 1855 beneath.

This token is a rude specimen of colonial workmanship.

Launceston (Tasmania.)

No. 101. Penny. Size 21. Common.

Obv: E. F. DEASE in centre. ONE above the name. PENNY beneath. WHOLESALE & RETAIL DRAPERY WAREHOUSE BRISBANE S$^{T.}$ around the token.

Rev: A golden fleece. SIC VOS NON VOBIS VELLERA FERTIS OVES (Thus ye sheep bear your fleeces not for yourselves)

This token does not bear the name of the town, but Brisbane St. is in Launceston. Both Neumann and Weyl describe it amongst the Hobart Town tokens.

No. 102. Halfpenny. Size 17. Common.

Same as preceding, excepting the word HALF on the obverse instead of ONE.

Melbourne (Victoria.)

No. 103. Penny. Size 21. Common.

Obv: A female seated on a bale; holding scales in right hand and cornucopia in left, out of which is issuing fruits and flowers. Cask at back. Water and ship in the distance. MELBOURNE VICTORIA in half circle above. 1858 beneath.

Rev: Australian Arms. The quartering on shield is a golden fleece, a ship, an ox, and an anchor. ADVANCE AUSTRALIA on scroll. PEACE & PLENTY in half circle above.

No. 104. Halfpenny. Size 17½. Common.

Obv: A Kangaroo standing facing right. MELBOURNE above. W. J. TAYLOR MEDALLIST | TO THE GREAT | EXHIBITION | 1851 in four straight lines of minute letters under the kangaroo.

Rev: Figure of Britannia seated facing left, holding an olive branch in right hand. Wand in left. AUSTRALIA in half circle above.

No. 105. Halfpenny. Size 17½. Common.

Obv: ADAMSON, WATTS, McKECHNIE & Co * around the token. WHOLESALE | & RETAIL | WAREHOUSEMEN in three straight lines in centre.

Rev: 11 COLLINS St. EAST * MELBOURNE * around the token. MAY 1st | 1855 in two straight lines in centre.

No. 106. Penny. Size 21. Common.

Obv: JOHN ANDREW & Co. ✱ IMPORTERS AND GENERAL DRAPERS ✱ around the token between the dotted edge and a dotted inner circle. 11 LONSDALE STREET WEST ✱ MELBOURNE ✱ forming a second circle, between the dotted circle and a plain inner circle, in the centre of which is a lion with small crown upon his head. Fore paw resting upon a shield. COARD—LONDON beneath the lion.

(This design is similar to No. 129. See also 124, 161 & 115, the latter No. being the earliest date of this design.)

Rev: Same as obverse of No. 103, excepting date, which is 1860.

No. 107. Halfpenny. Size 17½. Common.

Obv: and Rev: same as No. 106.

No. 108. Penny. Size 21. Common.

JNO. ANDREW & Co. | DRAPERS &c. in two lines in centre. 11 LONSDALE ST. WEST in half circle beneath. MELBOURNE above.

Rev: Kangaroo and Emu facing. VICTORIA above. 1862 beneath. COARD in minute letters beneath the emu. LONDON beneath the kangaroo.

No. 109. Halfpenny. Size 17½. Common.

Obv: and Rev: Same as No. 108.

No. 110. Penny. Size 21. Common.

Obv: I. BOOTH | ✱DRAPER✱ | OUTFITTER &c. | MELBOURNE | VICTORIA displayed in five lines.

Rev: Britannia seated, same as No. 90, but rather better executed.

No. 111. Halfpenny. Size 17½. Scarce.

Obv: CROMBIE CLAPPERTON & FINDLAY———41 | WEST | LONSDALE | STREET in four lines in centre.

Rev: Same as obverse of No. 104.

No. 112. Penny. Size 21. Common.

Obv: A. DAVIDSON | 112 | COLLINS St EAST | CORNER | OF | RUSSELL ST. | MELBOURNE displayed in seven lines within a circle in centre. GROCER WINE & SPIRIT MER-

C

CHANT : around the token between the inner circle and dotted edge.

Rev : Same as No. 35.

No. 113. Penny. Size 21. Common.

Obv : Same as No. 112.

Rev : Same as No. 37.

No. 114. Penny. Size 20½. Common.

Obv : EDWD. DE' CARLE & Co. in half circle above. AUCTIONEERS | &c. | in two straight lines in centre. MELBOURNE in half circle beneath.

Rev : Female seated facing left; holding scales in right hand and short sword in left. Shield at side. TASMANIA in half circle above. ✴ ANNO 1855 ✴ in half circle beneath.

No. 115. Penny. Size 21. Very common.

Obv : E. DE CARLE & Co. AUCTIONEERS & LAND AGENTS. around the token between the dotted edge and a dotted circle. QUEEN'S ROYAL ARCADE OFFICE ✴ between the dotted circle and a plain inner circle, in centre of which is a lion with small crown upon his head. Fore paw resting upon a shield.

(The design of this token is similar to No. 106. The name of the maker does not, however, appear upon it, and the foreground upon which the lion stands also varies slightly.)

Rev : Same as obverse of No. 103, excepting the date, which is 1855.

No. 116. Penny. Size 21. Common.

Obv : E. DE. CARLE & Co in half circle. GROCERS | & SPIRIT | MERCHANTS in three straight lines in centre. MELBOURNE & PLENTY VICTORIA . in half circle beneath.

Rev : Figure of Britannia seated same as No. 110, and apparently from the same die.

No. 117. Penny. Size 21. Common.

Obv : S. DEEBLE | DRAPER in two lines within a circle in centre—ornamental flourishes above the name, and between the name and beneath the word draper. LONDON HOUSE BOURKE St.: MELBOURNE : around the token between the dotted edge and the inner circle.

Rev : Same as No. 33.

No. 118. Penny. Size 21. Common.

Obv : Same as No. 117.

Rev : Same as No. 33, excepting that ADVANCE AUSTRALIA is on the scroll beneath the arms.

No. 119. Penny. Size 21. Common.

Obv : Same as No. 117.

Rev : Same as No. 172.

No. 120. Penny. Size 21. Common.

Obv : Same as No. 117.

Rev : Same as No. 174.

No. 121. Penny. Size 21. Common.

Obv : EVANS | & | FOSTER | 78 | BOURKE ST. | EAST in six straight lines in centre. BOOKSELLERS & STATIONERS in three parts of a circle above. : MELBOURNE : beneath.

Rev : Same as No. 39.

No. 122. Penny. Size 21. Scarce.

Obv : 225 KING STREET MELBOURNE . VICTORIA. Head of Queen Victoria similar to head on the English copper coins, in centre.

Rev : FENWICK BROTHERS IMPORTERS & CLOTHIERS . 225 KING St. A large flag staff, with cross stay and numerous ropes and tackle. A house at left side. FLAG STAFF beneath.

No. 123. Penny. Size 21. Scarce.

Obv : 225 KING STREET MELBOURNE . VICTORIA . Head of Queen Victoria slightly smaller than head on obverse of No. 122, and within a circle.

Rev : Same as No. 122.

No. 124. Penny. Size 21. Very common.

Obv : HIDE & DE CARLE . GROCERS & WINE MER- CHANTS around the token between the dotted edge and a dotted circle. ELIZABETH STREET . MELBOURNE . between the dotted circle and a plain inner circle, in centre of which is a lion with small crown upon his head and fore paw resting on a shield.

Rev : Female seated on a bale, eyes bandaged. Scales in right hand and cornucopia in left, out of which is issuing fruits and flowers. Cask at back. Water and ship in the distance. MELBOURNE . VICTORIA . in half circle above the figure. 1857 beneath.

No. 125. Halfpenny. Size 17½. Very common.

Obv : and Rev : same as No. 124.

No. 126. Penny. Size 21. Very common.

Varying only from No. 124 by date on the reverse, which is 1858.

No. 127. Halfpenny. Size 17½. Common.

Same as preceding (also 1858.)

No. 128. Penny. Size 21. Very common.

Obv : Same as No. 124.

Rev : Same as No. 126, excepting that the figures in the date (1858) are much larger, and the letters—MELBOURNE. VICTORIA are also larger, and there is no dot or stop after the word VICTORIA as in Nos. 124 & 126.

There are other varieties of this token. Weyl mentions 9, but with the exception of the five described, they vary only slightly in the position of the letters on the obverse design, and it would require a practised eye to detect that several dies were used in their manufacture.

No. 129. Penny. Size 21. Common.

Obv : A. G. HODGSON ✶ OUTFITTER AND TAILOR ✶ around the token between the dotted edge and a dotted circle.

13 LONSDALE STREET WEST ✸ MELBOURNE ✸ between the dotted circle and a plain inner circle, in centre of which is a lion with small crown upon his head and fore paw resting on a shield. COARD LONDON beneath the lion. (Same design as No. 106.)

Rev: Same as No. 106.

No. 130. Halfpenny. Size 17½. Common.
Obv: and Rev: same as preceding.

No. 131. Penny. Size 21. Common.
Obv: A. G. HODGSON | OUTFITTER | &c. in three lines in centre. 13 LONSDALE St. WEST in half circle beneath. MELBOURNE above.
Rev: Kangaroo and Emu facing. Same as 108.

No 132. Halfpenny. Size 17½. Common.
Obv: and Rev: same as preceding.

No. 133. Penny. Size 21. Common.
Obv: J. HOSIE | A Thistle with two leaves | 10 & 12 | BOURKE St. | EAST within a circle in centre. THE SCOTCH PIE SHOP : MELBOURNE : around the token between the dotted edge and inner circle.
Rev: Same as No. 118.

No. 134. Penny. Size 21. Common.
Obv: Same as No. 133.
Rev: Same as No. 118, excepting that the letters in the name of the maker (T. STOKES. MAKER. | 100 COLLINS ST. EAST. MELBOURNE) are much smaller, and there is a rose, two thistles, and two leaves of the shamrock above the scroll and beneath the shield.

No. 135. Penny. Size 21. Common.
Obv: Same as No. 133.
Rev: Same as No. 39.

No. 136. Penny. Size 21. Common.
Obv: Same as No. 133.
Rev: Same as No. 172.

No. 137. Penny. Size 21. Common.

 Obv : Same as No. 133.

 Rev : Same as No. 36.

No. 138. Halfpenny.

 Obv : THE ORIGINAL ✳ SCOTCH PIE SHOP ✳

 Rev : 12 BOURKE ST. EAST.

The description of this token is taken from Batty's Catalogue of the Copper Coinage of Great Britain. It is placed under "Scotland—Miscellaneous." There is no town given on the token, but it belongs to this series, although I have never met with a halfpenny of this issuers.

No. 139. Penny. Size 21. Common.

 Obv : ROBERT HYDE & Co. MELBOURNE around the token between the dotted edge and inner circle. GENERAL | MARINE | STORE | SHIPPERS OF | RAGS GLASS | METALS | &c. in seven lines within a circle in centre.

 Rev : Same as No. 103, with date 1857 beneath.

No. 140. Halfpenny. Size 17½. Common.

 Obv : and Rev : same as preceding.

No. 141. Penny. Size 21. Common.

 Same as No. 139, excepting date on reverse, which is 1861.

No. 142. Halfpenny. Size 17½. Common.

 Obv : and Rev : same as No. 141.

No. 143. Penny. Size 21. Scarce.

 . Obv : S & S. LAZARUS | WHOLESALE | AND RETAIL | FANCY REPOSITORY | 29, 30, 31, 69, 70 & 71 | QUEEN'S | ARCADE | MELBOURNE displayed in eight lines.

 Rev : IMPORTERS | OF | BIRMINGHAM | AND | SHEFFIELD | WARE | STATIONERY &c. displayed in seven lines.

No. 144. Penny. Size 21. Scarce.

 Obv : LEVY BROTHERS . ARCADE, MELBOURNE around the token between the dotted edge and dotted inner circle. IMPORTERS | OF | FANCY | GOODS in four lines within the circle in centre.

 Rev : Same as No. 22, excepting date, which is 1855.

No. 145. Penny. Size 21. Common.

Obv: J. McFARLANE | WHOLESALE AND RETAIL | GROCER in three lines in centre. CORNER OF ELIZABETH & LONSDALE S^{ts.} . MELBOURNE around the token.

Rev: A female standing, holding olive branch in right hand. To the right a lion. On the left a lamb. PEACE AND PLENTY in half circle above.

No. 146. Penny. Size 21. Common.

Obv: MILLER BROTHERS in half circle. COACH | BUILDERS in two straight lines. MELBOURNE in half circle beneath. In centre between the words COACH and BUILDERS is a representation of a vehicle known in the colonies as a " buggy."

Rev: Same as No. 33.

No. 147. Penny. Size 21. Common

Obv: Same as No 146.

Rev: Same as No. 39.

No. 148. Penny. Size 21. Common.

Obv: Same as No. 146

Rev: Same as No. 35.

No. 149. Penny. Size 21. Common.

Obv: Same as No. 146.

Rev: Same as No. 37.

No. 150. Penny. Size 21. Common.

Obv: MILLER & DISMOOR in half circle. DRAPERS | HABERDASHERS &c | COLLINS St in three straight lines in centre. MELBOURNE in half circle beneath.

Rev: ONE | PENNY | TOKEN in three straight lines. SMITH & KEMP BIRM^{M.} in minute letters beneath the word TOKEN.

No. 151. Penny. Size 21. Common.

Obv: MOUBRAY LUSH | & Co | DRAPERS | MEL-BOURNE displayed in four lines.

Rev: Same as No. 25.

No. 152. Penny. Size 21. Common.

Obv: :GEORGE NICHOLS: | OPPOSITE | CORNER | TO | POST | OFFICE displayed in six lines within a circle in centre. BOOKSELLER & STATIONER . MELBOURNE . around the token between the dotted edge and inner circle.

Rev: Same as No. 134.

No. 153. Halfpenny. Size 17½. Common.

Obv: JAMES NOKES in half circle. GROCER in straight line in centre. MELBOURNE beneath.

Rev: IN COMMEMORATION OF THE LANDING OF * ——SIR | CHARLES | HOTHAM | 22D JUNE | 1854 in five lines in centre.

This token is one of a few, commemorating an event in Australian history. Sir Charles Hotham was Governor of Victoria, from the 22nd of June, 1854, until his death, 31st December, 1855. He was buried at Melbourne Cemetery, where a handsome monument is raised to his memory. He held office during a stormy period, and whatever his faults were, he acted according to the dictates of his conscience, and his death was hastened by the troubles thrust upon him.

No. 154. Halfpenny. Size 17½. Common.

Obv: Same as No. 153.

Rev: Same as No. 104.

No. 155. Penny. Size 21. Common.

Obv: 67 LITTLE COLLINS STREET EAST | ESTATE AGENT | & MONEY | LENDER | HUGH PECK | HOTEL BROKER | & VALUATOR | ESTABLISHED | 1853 | MELBOURNE displayed in ten lines.

Rev: 67 LITTLE COLLINS STREET EAST | RENTS & DEBTS | COLLECTED | HUGH PECK | PROCESS SERVED | LEVIES FOR RENT | ESTABLISHED | 1853 | MELBOURNE displayed in nine lines.

No. 156. Penny. Size 21. Common.

Obv: Same as No. 155.

Rev: Same as No. 33.

No. 157. Penny. Size 21. Common.

Obv: GEO. PETTY | 157 | ELIZABETH St in three straight lines in centre. SMITHFIELD Co in half circle above. MELBOURNE in half circle beneath.

Rev: A well executed figure of Justice, facing front. Scales in right hand. Wand in left. VICTORIA above.

No. 158. Penny. Size 21. Common.

Obv: ROBISON BROs | & CO. | 31 | FLINDERS St | WEST displayed in five lines within a circle in centre. VICTORIA COPPER WORKS : MELBOURNE : between the dotted edge and inner circle.

Rev: Same as No. 39.

No. 159. Penny. Size 21. Common.

Obv: Same as No. 158.

Rev: Same as No. 172.

No. 160. Penny. Size 21. Common.

Obv: Same as No. 158.

Rev: Same as No. 169.

No. 161. Penny. Size 21. Common.

Obv: G & W. H. ROCKE. ENGLISH FURNITURE IM- PORTERS . around the token between the dotted edge and a dotted circle. 18 LONSDALE STREET EAST . MELBOURNE. in circular form between the dotted circle and a plain second circle, in centre of which is a lion with small crown upon his head, and fore paw resting on a shield.

Rev: Same as Obv: of No. 103, excepting date, which is 1859.

No. 162. Penny. Size 21. Common.

Obv: ANNAND SMITH & Co. in half circle. FAMILY | GROCERS in two straight lines in centre. . MELBOURNE . in half circle beneath.

Rev: Britannia seated, facing left, holding olive branch in right hand, and trident in left. Shield at side. Water and ship in the distance. BRITANNIA in half circle above.

No. 163. Penny. Size 21. Common.

Obv: Same as No. 162.

Rev: Same as No. 162, excepting that the olive branch has 11 leaves instead of 14, and there is a minute H & S at back of shield (Heaton & Sons.)

No. 164. Penny. Size 21. Common.

Obv: ✸ THOMAS STOKES MAKER ✸ in half circle above. 100 | COLLINS ST. | EAST in three lines in centre. MELBOURNE beneath.

Rev: Australian Arms. ADVANCE AUSTRALIA on scroll at foot. The shield is divided into quarters by several lines forming a cross; a star in centre, and four other stars, one at each extremity of the cross. The shield is quartered by a ship, a golden fleece, an anchor and a wheatsheaf. VICTORIA 1862 above. T. STOKES. MAKER. | 100 COLLINS ST. EAST. MELBOURNE in two lines forming a half circle beneath the arms. Beneath the scroll is a rose with two leaves, a thistle on each side of it, and a leaf of the shamrock at each extremity. (Same as No. 33, excepting that ADVANCE AUSTRALIA is on the scroll.)

No. 165. Penny. Size 21. Common.

Obv: Same as No. 164.

Rev: Same as No. 164, excepting that the name T STOKES. MAKER, 100 COLLINS ST. EAST. MELBOURNE is much smaller, and there is also a rose, two thistles, and two leaves of the shamrock above the scroll and beneath the shield. (Same as No. 134.)

No. 166. Penny. Size 21. Common.

Obv: Same as No. 164.

Rev: An Emu. Sun and rays at back. ADVANCE VICTORIA on scroll beneath the Emu. VICTORIA 1862 in half circle above. T. STOKES. MAKER. | 100 COLLINS ST. EAST MELBOURNE in two lines at foot.

No. 167. Penny. Size 21. Common.

Obv : T. STOKES | DIE | SINKER | SEAL ENGRAVER | LETTER CUTTER | CHECK & TOKEN | MAKER | MEL-BOURNE displayed in eight lines.

Rev : Same as No. 166.

No. 168. Halfpenny. Size 17½. Common.

Obv : Same as No. 167.

Rev : MILITARY ORNAMENT AND BUTTON MAKER : around the token, close to dotted edge. T. STOKES : 100 COLLINS ST. EAST MELBOURNE : around the token forming a second circle. ELECTRO | PLATING | AND | GILDING in four lines in centre.

No. 169. Penny. Size 21. Common.

Obv : T . STOKES | 100 | COLLINS ST | EAST | MEL-BOURNE displayed in five lines within a circle in centre. LETTER CUTTER BUTTON CHECK & TOKEN MAKER : around the token between the dotted edge and inner circle.

Rev : In centre a vine branch with grapes and leaves, partly surrounded by a circle. T. STOKES MAKER completing the circle. 100 COLLINS ST. EAST MELBOURNE in half circle beneath. VICTORIA 1862 above the vine branch.

No. 170. Penny. Size 21. Common.

Obv : T. STOKES | 100 | COLLINS ST. | EAST | MEL-BOURNE displayed in five lines within a circle in centre. LETTER CUTTER SEAL ENGRAVER TOKEN MAKER . around the token between the dotted edge and inner circle.

Rev : A vine branch with grapes and leaves. T. STOKES-MAKER-MEL in small letters beneath, the whole within a circle in centre. (The vine branch has eleven large leaves, two bunches of

grapes, and terminates with four small leaves.) VICTORIA.
1862: IN VINO VERITAS: around the token between the
dotted edge and inner circle.

No. 171. Penny. Size 21. Common.

Obv: Same as No. 170, excepting that after LETTER
CUTTER there is a dot, or stop: after SEAL ENGRAVER a
dot, and after TOKEN MAKER two dots—thus:

Rev: Same as No. 170, excepting that T. STOKES MAKER
MEL. is a trifle larger, and the vine branch varies, by having
nine large leaves, two bunches of grapes, and terminates with
four small leaves and a binder.

No. 172. Penny. Size 21. Common.

Obv: Same as No. 170.

Rev: Same as No. 166, excepting that beneath the scroll at
foot of Emu is a rose with two leaves, a thistle on each side of rose,
and a leaf of the shamrock at each extremity.

No. 173. Penny. Size 21. Common.

Obv: T. STOKES | 100 | COLLINS ST. | EAST. in four
lines in centre. MELBOURNE beneath. : BUTTON CHECK

& TOKEN MAKER : in three parts of a circle around the token above the name.

 Rev : Same as No. 166.

No. 174. Penny. Size 21. Common.

 Obv : T. STOKES | 100 | COLLINS ST. | EAST | MEL-BOURNE displayed in five lines within a circle in centre. MILITARY ORNAMENT BUTTON & TOKEN MAKER : around the token between the dotted edge and inner circle.

 Rev : A wheatsheaf in centre. ADVANCE AUSTRALIA in half circle above. 1862 beneath.

No. 175. Penny. Size 21. Common.

 Obv : Same as No. 174.

 Rev : Same as No. 171.

No. 176. Penny. Size 21. Common.

 (The following four tokens are of the same design, but vary in the number and disposition of the leaves on the vine branch on the reverse. They are all without the name of the maker.)

 Obv : A wheatsheaf in centre. ADVANCE AUSTRALIA in half circle above. 1862 beneath. (Same as Rev : of No. 174.)

 Rev : A vine branch within a circle in centre. VICTORIA 1862 : IN VINO VERITAS : around the token between the dotted edge and inner circle. The vine branch has sixteen leaves and two bunches of grapes, arranged thus :—Eleven large leaves, with bunch of grapes beneath the seventh and ninth leaf, small leaf above the ninth leaf, and small leaf above the eleventh leaf, terminating with three small leaves and a binder.

No. 177. Penny. Size 21. Common.

Obv : Same as No. 176.

Rev : Same as No. 176, excepting that the fourteen leaves on the vine branch are arranged thus :—Eleven large leaves, with bunch of grapes under the sixth leaf and eleventh leaf, terminating with three small leaves and a binder.

No. 178. Penny. Size 21. Common.

Obv : Same as No. 176.

Rev : Same as No. 176, excepting in the disposition of the leaves on the vine branch, which has fourteen leaves, and two bunches of grapes, arranged thus :—Eight large leaves : beneath the fifth leaf and eighth leaf a bunch of grapes, a small leaf above the eighth leaf, followed by a large leaf, and terminating with four small leaves and a binder.

No. 179. Penny. Size 21. Common.

Obv : Same as No. 176.

Rev : Same as No. 176, excepting that the vine branch has fourteen leaves and two bunches of grapes arranged thus :—Nine large leaves : beneath the sixth and ninth leaves a bunch of grapes, above the ninth leaf a small leaf, terminating with four small leaves and a binder.

No. 180. Penny. Size 21. Common.

(The following four tokens, having for an obverse arms as shown in engraving of reverse of No. 33, again vary only in the reverse by the number and disposition of the leaves on the vine branch.)

Obv : Australian Arms same as reverse of No. 33.

Rev : Same as No. 176

No. 181. Penny. Size 21. Common.

    Obv : Same as No. 180.

    Rev : Same as No. 176, excepting that the leaves on the vine branch vary. The branch has fourteen leaves, arranged in the following order:—Ten large leaves, a bunch of grapes under the seventh leaf and tenth leaf, terminating with four small leaves and a binder.

No. 182. Penny. Size 21. Common.

    Obv : Same as No. 180.

    Rev : Same as No. 176, excepting that the arrangement of the fourteen leaves on the vine branch differ thus :—Nine large leaves, beneath the fifth and eighth leaves a bunch of grapes, small leaf above the eighth leaf, followed by a large leaf and four small leaves and a binder.

No. 183. Penny. Size 21. Common.

    Obv : Same as No. 180.

    Rev : Same as No. 179.

No. 184. Halfpenny. Size 17½. Common.

    Obv : T. W. THOMAS & Co. in half circle above. GROCERS : in straight line in centre. * MELBOURNE * in half circle beneath.

    Rev : Same as No. 153.

No. 185. Halfpenny. Size 17½. Common.

    Obv : THRALE & CROSS in half circle. FAMILY | GROCERY | & | EGG POWDER | STORE in five straight lines in centre. HOWARD St. NORTH MELBOURNE in half circle beneath.

    Rev : Same as obverse of No. 104.

No. 186. Halfpenny. Size 17½. Common.

    Obv : Same as No. 185.

    Rev : Same as reverse of No. 104.

No. 187. Penny. Size 21. Common.

    Obv : T. WARBURTON | 11 | LITTLE | BOURKE ST. | WEST | displayed in five lines within a circle in centre. IRON &

ZINC SPOUTING WORKS: MELBOURNE: around the token between the dotted edge and inner circle.

Rev: Same as No. 33.

No. 188. Penny. Size 21. Common.

Obv: Same as No. 187.

Rev: Same as No. 174.

No. 189. Penny. Size 21. Common.

Obv: Same as No. 187.

Rev: Same as No. 39.

No. 190. Penny. Size 21. Common.

Obv: Same as No. 187.

Rev: Same as No. 169.

No. 191. Penny. Size 21. Common.

Obv: Same as No. 187.

Rev: Same as No. 171.

No. 192. Penny. Size 21. Common.

Obv: Female seated on a bale, eyes bandaged, holding scales in right hand, and horn of plenty in left, out of which is issuing fruits and flowers. Cask at back. Water and ship in the distance. WARNOCK BROS. MELBOURNE & above. MALDON beneath.

Rev: Australian Arms, same as No. 103, excepting date 1861 is beneath the scroll.

No. 193. Penny. Size 19. Common.

(This token is in bronze, and of the same weight and size as the English penny of the period.)

Obv: Same as preceding, excepting that the & is omitted after the word MELBOURNE.

Rev: Same as preceding (No. 192), excepting date, which is 1863.

Morpeth (New South Wales).

No. 194. Penny. Size 21. Common.

Obv: JAMES CAMPBELL in half circle above, GENERAL | STORES in two curved lines in centre · MORPETH · beneath.

Rev: Same as No. 25.

No. 195. Halfpenny. Size 17½. Common.

    Obv: and Rev: Same as preceding.

New Town (Tasmania).

No. 196. Penny. Size 21. Common.

    Obv: A view of the Toll House and Gate in centre. NEW TOWN TOLL GATE in half circle above, ✱ R. JOSEPHS ✱ beneath.

    Rev: Female seated on bale. Cask at back. Scales in right hand, horn of plenty in left. Water and ship in the distance. VAN DIEMANS LAND in half circle above, 1855 beneath.

No. 197. Halfpenny. Size 17½. Common.

    Obv: and Rev: Same as preceding.

Port Albert (Victoria).

No. 198. Penny. Size 21. Common.

    GIPPS LAND: HARDWARE COMPANY: around the token, between the dotted edge and an inner circle, PORT | ALBERT | & | SALE in four straight lines within the inner circle.

    Rev: Same as No. 33.

No. 199. Penny. Size 21. Common.

    Obv: Same as No. 198.

    Rev: A Plough in centre. TRADE & AGRICULTURE in half circle above. T. STOKES MAKER | 100 COLLINS ST. EAST MELBOURNE in two circular lines beneath the plough.

Queensland.

No. 200. Penny. Size 21. Common.

    Obv: MERRY & BUSH in half circle. QUEENSLAND in curved line in centre. 1863 beneath. ·MERCHANTS & GENERAL IMPORTERS· around the token.

    Rev: Same as No. 103.

Richmond (Victoria).

No. 201. Penny. Size 21. Common.

Obv: BARROWCLOUGH in half circle. 100 | BRIDGE | ROAD in three straight lines within a circle in centre. BOOK-SELLER & STATIONER ✱ RICHMOND ✱ around the token between the dotted edge and inner circle.

Rev: Same as No. 134.

No. 202. Penny. Size 21. Common.

Obv: R. B. RIDLER | 187 | BRIDGE | ROAD | RICH-MOND displayed in five lines within a circle in centre. WHOLESALE & RETAIL BUTCHER: around the token between the dotted edge and inner circle.

Rev: same as No. 33.

No. 203. Penny. Size 21. Common.

Obv: Same as No. 202.

Rev: Same as No. 39.

No. 204. Penny. Size 21. Common.

Obv: Same as No. 202.

Rev: Same as No. 174.

Rockhampton (Queensland.)

No. 205. Penny. Size 21. Scarce.

Obv: BELL | & | GARDNER in three lines in centre. ✱ IRONMONGERS ✱ in half circle above. ROCKHAMPTON in half circle beneath.

Rev: A wreath of Colonial flowers surmounted by the rising sun. PENNY | TOKEN in two lines in centre.

This token is apparently of Colonial workmanship.

No. 206. Penny. Size 21. Common.

Obv: QUEENSLAND STORES in half circle above. ROCK-HAMPTON in straight line in centre. D. T. MULLIGAN in half circle beneath.

Rev: Same as No. 42.

No. 207. Halfpenny. Size 17½. Common.

Obv: and Rev: same as preceding.

Sale (Victoria.)—See also Port Albert.

No. 208. Penny. Size 21. Scarce.

Obv: JAs. DAVEY | & Co. | GIPPS LAND | STORE | FOSTER ST. | SALE displayed in six lines within a circle in centre. WHOLESALE & RETAIL DRAPERS GROCERS & IMPORTERS: around the token between the dotted edge and inner circle.

Rev: Same as No. 33.

No. 209. Penny. Size 21. Scarce.

Obv: J. D. LEESON : WATCHMAKER & JEWELLER : around the token between the dotted edge and inner circle. FANCY | MUSEUM | SALE in three lines within a circle in centre.

Rev: Same as No. 33.

Sandhurst (Victoria.)—See also Bendigo.

No. 210. Penny. Size 21. Scarce.

Obv: STEAD BROTHERS | FRUITERERS | GROCERS | & SEEDSMEN | PALL MALL | SANDHURST displayed in six lines.

Rev: Same as No. 33.

No. 211. Penny. Size 21. Scarce.

Obv: Same as No. 210.

Rev: Same as No. 37.

Sandridge (Victoria.)

No. 212. Penny. Size 21. Scarce.

Obv: SUGAR COMPANIES TREACLE DELIVERED partly around the token between the dotted edge, and three parts of an inner circle. ODD FELLOWS STORE | in half circle. W. C. COOK | BAY ST. | SANDRIDGE circular. The last four lines in centre. ORDERS PUNCTUALLY | ATTENDED TO arranged in two lines at foot so as to complete the inner circle.

Rev: Same as No. 33.

South Yarra (Victoria.)

No. 213. Penny. Size 21. Common.

Obv: THOs. H. COPE | GENERAL | DRAPER displayed in three lines within a circle in centre. GARDENERS CREEK ROAD : SOUTH YARRA : around the token between the dotted edge and inner circle.

Rev: Same as No. 33.

No. 214. Halfpenny. Size 17½. Common.

Obv: FISHER | DRAPER | MARLBOROUGH | HOUSE | GARDINERS CREEK ROAD displayed in five lines.

Rev: Kangaroo and emu facing. AUSTRALIA above. 1857 beneath.

Sydney (New South Wales.)

No. 215. Penny. Size 21. Common.

Obv: BATTLE | & | WEIGHT in three lines within a circle in centre. 81 & 83 SOUTH HEAD ROAD SYDNEY DRAPERS &c. around the token between the dotted edge and inner circle.

Rev: Female standing facing left, holding scales in right hand and horn of plenty in left, out of which is issuing fruits and flowers. Water and ship in the distance.

No. 216. Penny. Size 20½. Common.

Obv : FLAVELLE BROs. & Co. · SYDNEY & BRISBANE · around the token. ONE | PENNY in two straight lines in centre.

Rev : Kangaroo and Emu facing. W J TAYLOR beneath the Emu. LONDON beneath the Kangaroo. Same as No. 260.

No. 217. Penny. Size 20½. Common.

Obv : FLAVELLE BROs. & Co. in half circle above. ONE | PENNY in two lines beneath. OPTICIANS & JEWELLERS | · SYDNEY & BRISBANE · in two half circular lines beneath the words one penny.

Rev : Same as No. 216.

No. 218. Penny. Size 21. Common.

Obv : HANKS | AND | COMPY. in three straight lines in centre. · AUSTRALIAN TEA MART · in half circle above. SYDNEY beneath.

Rev : Same as No. 103, excepting date 1857 beneath the Arms.

No. 219. Halfpenny. Size 17½. Common.

Obv : and Rev : Same as No. 218.

No. 220. Penny. Size 21. Common.

Obv : HANKS | AND | LLOYD in three straight lines in centre. AUSTRALIAN TEA MART in half circle above, · SYDNEY · beneath.

Rev : TO COMMEMORATE THE OPENING OF around the token. THE | SYDNEY | RAILWAY | 26TH SEPTR. in four lines in centre. · 1855 · beneath.

No. 221. Halfpenny. Size 17½. Common.

Obv : and Rev : Same as preceding.

No. 222. Penny. Size 21. Common.

Obv : Same as No. 220.

Rev : Same as No. 218.

No. 223. Penny. Size 21. Common.

Obv : and Rev : Same as preceding, excepting that the formation of the letters vary, most noticeable in the word SYDNEY, the letters of which are more elongated than on the previous token.

No. 224. Halfpenny. Size 17½. Common.

Obv: and Rev: Same as preceding.

No. 225. Halfpenny. Size 17½. Common.

This token is of similar design to No. 224, but varies in its details. There being no dots before and after the word SYDNEY and the word AND between the name (Hanks and Lloyd) is much larger.

No. 226. Penny. Size 21. Common.

Obv: IRON MERCHANTS AND GENERAL IRON-MONGERS around the token between the dotted edge and inner circle. ESTABLISHED | 1820 | IREDALE & Co. | SYDNEY . displayed in four lines within a circle in centre.

Rev: Britannia seated facing left, holding Olive branch in right hand, and Trident in left. Shield at side. Water and Ship in the distance. BRITANNIA in half circle above. H & S in minute letters on rock at back of shield. (Heaton & Sons.)

The design on the reverse of this token is precisely similar to the design on the reverse of the English penny of King George III., 1806.

No. 227. Penny. Size 21. Very common.

Obv: Same as No. 226.

Rev: Female standing facing left, eyes bandaged; holding scales in right hand and horn of plenty in left, out of which is issuing fruits and flowers. Water and Ship in the distance. AUSTRALIA above the figure.

No. 228. Penny. Size 21. Very common.

Obv: Same as No. 227, excepting that the letters are more extended, particularly noticeable in the word ESTABLISHED.

Rev: Same as No. 227.

No. 229. Penny. Size 21. Very common.

Obv: Same as No. 227, excepting that the word ESTABLISHED is thicker, heavier, and more extended, the date (1820) is larger, and the word SYDNEY is in what a printer would call an elongated letter.

Rev: Same as No. 227.

There are several other varieties of this token with precisely similar wording, but varying slightly in the formation of the letters. The three specimens chosen (Nos. 227, 228, and 229) are probably those showing the greatest variation, but from the number of dies used in the manufacture of this, without doubt, the largest issue of the series, it is somewhat difficult to make a fairly representative selection.

No. 230. Penny. Size 21. Common.

Obv: J. M. LEIGH | TOBACCONIST | 524 GEORGE STREET | SYDNEY displayed in four lines.

Rev: Britannia seated, similar to No. 226.

No. 231. Penny. Size 19. Common.

Obv: J. MACGREGOR | 320, | GEORGE STREET | SYDNEY displayed in four lines within a dotted circle in centre. THE CITY TEA WAREHOUSE ✱ ✱ ✱ around the token, between the dotted edge and dotted inner circle.

Rev: Australian Arms within a dotted circle in centre. ESTABLISHED in half circle above. 1855 beneath. THE SULTAN'S STEAM COFFEE WORKS ✱ SYDNEY ✱ around the token between the dotted edge and dotted inner circle.

No. 232. Halfpenny. Size 16. Common.

Obv: and Rev: same as preceding.

No. 233. Penny. Size 21. Common.

Obv: METCALFE | & | LLOYD | 478 GEORGE St | SYDNEY displayed in five lines in centre. SHIPPING AND FAMILY GROCERS in three parts of a circle above.

Rev: WINE | AND | SPIRIT | MERCHANTS in four lines in centre. PURVEYORS OF THE CONCENTRATED FAMILY COFFEE—1863 around the token.

No. 234. Halfpenny. Size 17½. Common.

Obv: and Rev: same as preceding.

No. 235. Penny. Size 21. Common.

Obv: B. PALMER | PITT & KING St | SYDNEY in three lines in centre. WHOLESALE in half circle above. WINE & SPIRIT DEPOT in half circle beneath.

Rev: A bird (the liver) holding an olive branch in its mouth. LIVERPOOL above. ARMS beneath.

No. 236. Penny. Size 21. Common.

Obv: SMITH, PEATE & Co | GROCERS | TEA DEALERS | & | WINE MERCHANTS | 258 & 260 | GEORGE St | SYDNEY displayed in eight lines.

Rev: Female facing left, holding scales in right hand and cornucopia in left. Water and ship in the distance. ESTAB-LISHED above. 1836 beneath.

No. 237. Halfpenny. Size 17½. Common.

Obv: and Rev: same as preceding.

No. 238. Penny. Size 21. Scarce.

Obv: A view of the Stores. 424 over door. In the rear a second building, on which is TEA | STORES | STEAM | COFFEE | MILLS in five lines. ESTABLISHED | 1835 | SYDNEY in three lines beneath the building. J. C. T. in small letters at foot. (J. C. Thornthwaite Sydney.)

Rev: Britannia seated facing left. Helmeted. Trident in left hand, right hand resting on shield. BRITANNIA above. 1852 beneath. (The figure of Britannia is similar in design to the Britannia on the reverse of the English copper coinage of the period.)

No. 239. Halfpenny. Size 17½. Scarce.

Obv: and Rev: same as preceding.

No. 240. Penny. Size 21. Scarce.

Obv: Same as No. 238, excepting that the arrangement of the words on the building at the rear vary—TEA | STORES | STEAM |

COFFEE MILL | in four lines. ESTABLISHED 1835 | SYDNEY in two lines beneath front building.

Rev : Same as No. 238.

No. 241. Penny. Size 21. Scarce.

Obv : Same as No. 238.

Rev : Same as No. 238, excepting date, which is 1853.

No. 242. Penny. Size 22. Scarce.

Obv : J. C. THORNTHWAITE.—BOURKE STREET SURRY HILLS · around the token. DIE SINKER | a floral device of rose, thistle and shamrock | AND | a rose and three leaves | MEDALLIST arranged within a circle in centre.

Rev : Australian Arms. ADVANCE AUSTRALIA in half circle above. 1854 beneath.

No. 243. Halfpenny. Size 17½. Scarce.

Obv : Same as No. 242.

Rev : Australian Arms. SYDNEY · NEW SOUTH WALES in half circle above. 1854 beneath.

No. 244. Penny. Size 21. Very common.

Obv : A. TOOGOOD | MERCHANT | PITT & KING St. | SYDNEY displayed in four lines.

Rev : Same as No. 22, excepting date, which is 1855.

No. 245. Penny. Size 21. Common.

Obv : WEIGHT | AND | JOHNSON | DRAPERS | & | OUTFITTERS displayed in six lines in centre. LIVERPOOL & LONDON HOUSE in half circle above. · PITT STREET SYDNEY · in half circle beneath.

Rev : Same as No. 215.

No. 246. Halfpenny. Size 17½. Common.

Obv : WEIGHT & JOHNSON | DRAPERS | &c | LIVER-POOL | & | LONDON HOUSE | 249 & 251 PITT ST | SYDNEY displayed in eight lines.

Rev : Same as No. 215.

No. 247. Penny. Size 20. Scarce.

Obv : Head (probably of one of the makers) to left. WHITTY & BROWN MAKERS in half circle above. SYDNEY beneath.

Rev: Female standing facing left, holding scales in right hand and cornucopia in left, out of which is issuing fruits and flowers. Water and ship in the distance. NEW SOUTH WALES in half circle above.

No. 248. Penny. Size 21. Scarce.

Obv: A ram in centre. · PEACE AND PLENTY · SYDNEY · N.S.W · around the ram.

Rev: Same as No. 247.

No. 249. Penny. Size 20. Scarce.

Obv: ONE | PENNY in two lines within a circle in centre. ADVANCE AUSTRALIA ✱ ✱ ✱ around the token between the dotted edge and inner circle.

Rev: Same as No. 247.

Toowoomba (Queensland.)

No. 250. Penny. Size 21. Common.

Obv : T. F. MERRY & Co in half circle above. GENERAL | MERCHANTS in two straight lines in centre. TOOWOOMBA in half circle beneath.

Rev : Same as No. 103.

No. 251. Halfpenny. Size 17½. Common.

Obv : and Rev : same as preceding.

Wagga Wagga (New South Wales.)

No. 252. Penny. Size 21. Common.

Obv : LOVE & ROBERTS in straight line across centre. STOREKEEPERS in half circle, also in centre. WAGGA WAGGA in half circle above. NEW SOUTH WALES in half circle beneath.

Rev : A plough in centre. T STOKES MELBOURNE | 1865 beneath the plough. THE COMMERCIAL PASTORAL & FARMING INTERESTS : around the token.

Warrnambool (Victoria.)

No. 253. Penny. Size 21. Common.

Obv : WILLIAM BATEMAN JUNR. & Co WARNAMBOOL around an inner circle in centre. VICTORIA in straight line across centre. IMPORTERS AND GENERAL MERCHANTS . 1855 . around the token between the dotted edge and inner circle.

Rev : Same as No. 25.

No. 254. Penny. Size 21. Common.

Obv : W. W. JAMIESON | & Co | STOREKEEPERS in three straight lines in centre. LIEBEG STREET in half circle above. WARRNAMBOOL in half circle beneath.

Rev : Same as No. 25, excepting that date 1862 is beneath the figure.

Westbury (Tasmania.)

No. 255. Penny. Size 21. Common.

Obv : THOMAS WHITE in half circle above. AND | SON

in two lines in centre. · WESTBURY · in half circle beneath.

Rev: A kangaroo and emu facing. TASMANIA in half circle above. 1855 beneath.

No. 256. Halfpenny. Size 17½. Common.

Obv: and Rev: same as preceding.

No. 257. Penny. Size 21. Common.

Obv: Same as No. 253.

Rev: Same as No. 253, excepting date, which is 1857.

Wollongong (New South Wales.)

No. 258. Penny. Size 21. Common.

Obv: W. F. & D. L. LLOYD | DRAPERS GROCERS | WINE | & SPIRIT | MERCHANTS | WOLLONGONG displayed in six lines.

Rev: COLONIAL PRODUCE | TAKEN IN (1859) EXCHANGE around the token between the dotted edge and inner circle. Australian Arms within a circle in centre. (Golden fleece, ship, ox, and anchor on shield.)

No. 259. Halfpenny. Size 17½. Common.

Obv: and Rev: same as preceding.

MISCELLANEOUS.

No. 260. Penny. Size 21. Common.

Obv: Same as No. 249. ,

Rev: A kangaroo and emu facing. Kangaroo to right, emu to left. w. j. TAYLOR beneath the emu. LONDON beneath the kangaroo.

No. 261. Penny. Size 21. Common.

Obv: Same as reverse of 103, with date, 1859 beneath.

Rev: Female seated on a bale; eyes bandaged, holding scales in right hand and horn of plenty in left, out of which is issuing fruits and flowers. Cask at back. Water and ship in the distance. 1859 beneath.

No. 262. Penny. Size 21. Common.

Obv: THE AUSTRALIAN | TOKENS | MANUFACTURED BY T POPE & Co. | (COIN & PRESS MAKERS, | ST. PAUL'S SQR. | BIRMINGHAM,) | ARE VERY PROFITABLE | TO EXPORT displayed in nine lines.

Rev: Britannia seated facing right. Olive branch in right hand, trident in left. Shield at side. Water and ship in the distance. BRITANNIA in half circle above.

No. 263. Penny. Size 21½. Common.

Obv: Head of Professor Holloway to left. PROFESSOR—HOLLOWAY around the head. LONDON beneath the neck.

Rev: Female seated between two pillars. Serpent coiled partly around the pillar to right. HOLLOWAY'S PILLS AND OINTMENT in three parts of a circle above the figure. 1857 in exergue.

No. 264.   Halfpenny.   Size 18.   Common.
    Obv: and Rev: same as preceding.

No. 265.   Penny.   Size 21½.   Common.
    Obv: Same as No. 263.
    Rev: Same as No. 263, excepting date, which is 1858.

No. 266.   Halfpenny.   Size 18.   Common.
    Obv: and Rev: same as preceding.

NEW ZEALAND.

No. 267. Penny. Size 21. Common.

Obv: ALLIANCE TEA COMPANY | in half circle. OPPOSITE | BANK OF | NEW ZEALAND | ROBERT THOMPSON | MANAGER | 1866 displayed in seven lines.

Rev: TEAS COFFEES FRUITS & SPICES · 1866 · around the token. ITALIAN | WAREHOUSE | FANCY | GOODS in four straight lines in centre.

Auckland.

No. 268. Halfpenny. Size 17½. Common.

Obv: H. ASHTON | IMPORTER | OF | HABERDASHERY | & | TAILORS | TRIMMINGS | QUEEN St. AUCKLAND displayed in eight lines.

Rev: Female seated on a bale. Eyes bandaged; holding scales in right hand and horn of plenty in left, out of which is issuing fruits and flowers. Water and ship in the distance. NEW ZEALAND in half circle above the figure. 1858 beneath.

No. 269. Halfpenny. Size 17½. Common.

Obv: and Rev; same as preceding, excepting date, which is 1859.

No. 270. Penny. Size 21. Common.

Obv: Same as No. 268.

Rev: Female standing facing left. Eyes bandaged; holding scales in right hand and horn of plenty in left, out of which is issuing fruits and flowers. Water and ship in the distance. NEW ZEALAND above the figure. 1862 beneath.

No. 271. Penny. Size 21. Common.

Obv: and Rev: same as preceding, excepting date which is 1863.

No. 272. Penny. Size 19. Scarce.

Obv: Head of Queen to left, within a dotted circle in centre. VICTORIA in half circle above. · BORN MAY 24 1819 · beneath.

Rev: AUCKLAND LICENSED VICTUALLERS ASSOCIA-TION · around the token between the dotted edge and dotted inner circle. ESTABLISHED IN | NEW | ZEALAND | APRIL 4 | 1871 displayed in five lines within the inner circle.

No. 273. Penny. Size 21. Common.

Obv: CHARLES C. BARLEY in half circle above. WHOLESALE | GROCER | AUCKLAND in three straight lines in centre. NEW ZEALAND in half circle beneath.

Rev: Female seated on a bale. Eyes bandaged; holding with left hand cornucopia (horn of plenty), out of which is issuing fruits and flowers. Cask at back. Water and ship in the distance. GOD SAVE THE QUEEN in half circle above the figure. 1858 beneath.

No. 274. Penny. Size 21. Common.

Obv: ARCHIBALD CLARK—DRAPER around the token between the dotted edge and dotted inner circle. SHORTLAND | STREET | AUCKLAND displayed in three lines within the dotted inner circle.

Rev: Same as No. 268, excepting date, which is 1857.

No. 275. Penny. Size 21½. Scarce.

Obv: Full faced portrait and bust in centre. SAMUEL COOMBES above. MANUFACTURING CLOTHIER in half circle beneath. QUEEN ST. on right side of head. AUCKLAND on left.

Rev: TAILOR, OUTFITTER | QUEEN STREET | AUCKLAND | S. COOMBES | ALBERT STREET | GRAHAM TOWN | GENTLEMEN'S MERCER displayed in seven lines.

No. 276. Penny. Size 21. Common.

Obv: T S. FORSAITH · WHOLESALE & RETAIL DRAPER · around the token between the dotted edge and inner circle. MANCHESTER | HOUSE | · AUCKLAND · displayed in three lines within the circle in centre.

Rev: Same as No. 268.

No. 277. Halfpenny. Size 17½. Common.

Obv: and Rev: same as preceding.

No. 278. Penny. Size 21. Common.

Obv: B. GITTOS | LEATHER | MERCHANT | IM-PORTER OF | BOOTS & SHOES | &c. &c. in six lines.

Rev: WHOLESALE & RETAIL | LEATHER | & | GRINDERY | STORES | WYNDHAM STREET | AUCKLAND | N.Z. | 1864 displayed in nine lines.

No. 279. Penny. Size 20. Scarce.

Obv: R. GRATTEN in straight line across centre. THAMES HOTEL in half circle above. AUCKLAND in half circle beneath the name.

Rev: In centre a Maori paddling in canoe. 1872 beneath. The whole is surrounded by two branches of palm tree fern in the form of a wreath.

No. 280. Penny. Size 21. Scarce.

Obv: HOLLAND & BUILER ✱ 28 & 30 VICTORIA St. AUCKLAND ✱ around the token between the dotted edge and inner circle. OIL, COLOR | & | GLASS | MERCHANTS arranged in four lines within the outline of a painter's palate, within the circle in centre. STOKES & MARTIN in minute letters above the palate. MELBOURNE beneath.

Rev: IMPORTERS | OF | PAPERHANGINGS | GILT MOULDINGS | GLASS SHADES|&|PAINTERS MATERIALS displayed in seven lines.

No. 281. Penny. Size 19. Scarce.

Obv: MORRIS MARKS | PAWNBROKER | AND | SALESMAN | CORNER OF QUEEN St. | WELLESLEY St. | AUCKLAND displayed in seven lines.

Rev: Three balls within a circle in centre.

No. 282. Penny. Size 21. Common.

Obv: A palm tree in centre. MORRIN & Co. | QUEEN STREET in two lines above. AUCKLAND beneath. GROCERS, WINE & SPIRIT MERCHANTS in circular form, three parts around the token, beneath the tree.

Rev: Female standing facing left. Eyes bandaged. Scales in right hand, horn of plenty in left, out of which is issuing fruits and flowers. In the background a Maori with spear, and a gold digger with pick, joining hands. ADVANCE AUCKLAND in half circle above.

No. 283. Penny. Size 21. Common.

Obv: S. HAGUE SMITH between two lines across centre. MERCHANT | AUCKLAND in two lines beneath. WHOLE-SALE & RETAIL | IRONMONGER in two lines above the name.

Rev: A well executed head of the Prince Consort to left. PRINCE ALBERT above. BORN AUGᵀ 26 1819 DIED DIED DECᴿ 14 1861 in three parts of a circle beneath.

No. 284. Penny. Size 21. Common.

Obv: M. SOMERVILLE | WHOLESALE | FAMILY GROCER | CITY MART | AUCKLAND displayed in five lines.

Rev: A prettily designed device of a rose, thistle, and sham-rock, tied together by a ribbon. NEW ZEALAND above, 1857 beneath.

A design similar to the above appears on the reverse of a token issued by William Hodgins, Banker, Cloghjordan, with the word IRELAND over the rose, thistle, and shamrock, and 1858 beneath. Neumann in his valuable work has described this in the Australian series, and for some time I felt inclined to side with him and treat it as Australian, owing to the date of issue, the spelling of Clough-jordan (the letter u being omitted on the token), and its size, weight, and general appearance. However, the doubt was dispelled by a gentleman in Ireland, who, very kindly, in reply to my enquiries, informed me that William Hodgins was, in 1858, a

Banker at Cloughjordan, but has now emigrated to America, and that at the date the tokens in question circulated freely in the county of Tipperary.

No. 285. Penny. Size 21½. Scarce.

Obv: Head of Queen to left. VICTORIA DEI GRATIA. 1874.

Rev: UNITED SERVICE | HOTEL within a circle in centre. CORNER OF QUEEN & WELLESLEY STREETS · AUCKLAND, N.Z · around the token, between the dotted edge and inner circle.

No. 286. Penny. Size 21. Scarce.

Obv: EDWARD WATERS in straight line across centre. QUEEN ST. | AUCKLAND in two lines beneath. WHOLESALE & RETAIL | CONFECTIONER in two half circular lines above the name.

Rev: Head and draped bust of Maori to right. ONE PENNY TOKEN around the head. STOKES & MARTIN MELBOURNE in minute letters beneath the bust.

Christchurch.

No. 287. Penny. Size 21. Scarce.

Obv: J. CARO | & CO. | HIGH ST. arranged in three lines within a circle in centre. GENERAL IRONMONGERS : CHRISTCHURCH : around the token, between the dotted edge and inner circle.

Rev: A man guiding a plough. TRADE AND—AGRICULTURE around the figure. STOKES MELB at foot.

No. 288. Penny. Size 21. Common.

Obv: S. CLARKSON | BUILDER | & | IMPORTER | CASHEL STREET | CHRIST | CHURCH | NEW ZEALAND arranged in eight lines.

Rev: Female seated on a cask. Scales in right hand, horn of plenty in left. Water and ship in the distance. NEW ZEALAND above. 1875 beneath.

No. 289. Penny. Size 21. Common.

Obv: **T. W. GOURLAY & Co.** | IMPORTERS | OF in three lines above a stove, in centre. AND | KITCHENERS | CHRIST-CHURCH in three lines beneath the stove.

Rev: ECONOMY HOUSE—HIGH STREET around the token. BUILDERS | & | FURNISHING | IRONMONGERY in four lines. A saw in centre, between the words furnishing and ironmongery.

No. 290. Penny. Size 21. Common.

Obv: HENRY J. HALL— * CHRISTCHURCH COFFEE MILLS * around the token. ONE | PENNY in two lines between two lines in centre.

Rev: FAMILY GROCER— * WINE & SPIRIT MER-CHANT * around the token. H. J. HALL in straight line between two lines in centre.

No. 291. Halfpenny. Size 17½. Scarce.

Obv : Same as No. 290, excepting that HALF | PENNY is in two lines in centre.

Rev : Same as No. 290.

No. 292. Penny. Size 21. Common.

Obv : * H. J. HALL * in straight line between two lines in centre. CHRISTCHURCH in half circle above. COFFEE MILLS in half circle beneath.

Rev : Same as No. 290.

No. 293. Penny. Size 21. Common.

Obv: H. J. HALL in straight line across centre. : FAMILY . GROCER : in half circle above. WINE & SPIRIT MERCHANT in half circle beneath.

Rev: H. J. HALL in straight line across centre. CHRIST-CHURCH in half circle above. COFFEE MILLS in half circle beneath.

No. 294. Penny. Size 21.

Obv : Same as No. 290.

Rev : Same as No. 260.

This token has not been in circulation, and is evidently a mule.

No. 295. Halfpenny. Size 17½.

Obv : Same as reverse of No. 290.

Rev : Same as obverse of No. 102.

A mule—never in circulation.

No 296. Halfpenny. Size 17½.

Obv : Same as 290 and 291.

Rev : Same as No. 321.

A mule—never in circulation.

No. 297. Penny. Size 21. Common.

Obv : HOBDAY & JOBBERNS | DRAPERS | WATERLOO | HOUSE | · CHRISTCHURCH · displayed in five lines.

Rev : Arms of the province of Canterbury. ADVANCE CANTERBURY on scroll beneath the shield. STOKES & MARTIN MELBOURNE in minute letters at foot.

No. 298. Penny. Size 21. Common.

Obv : W. PETERSEN : HIGH ST. CHRISTCHURCH : around the token, between the dotted edge and inner circle. WATCHMAKER in half circle. AND in straight line in centre. · JEWELLER · in half circle beneath. The last three words within the circle in centre.

Rev : EVERYTHING SOLD GUARANTEED | ALL REPAIRS WELL EXECUTED in two lines, three parts around the upper portion of token. A prize cup and timepiece in centre. A watch face beneath. T. STOKES MELBOURNE in small letters beneath the watch.

No. 299. Penny. Size 21. Common.

Obv : WILLIAM PRATT | DIRECT | IMPORTER | OF | EVERY DESCRIPTION | OF LINEN DRAPERY | AND | CLOTHING displayed in eight lines.

Rev : ESTABLISHED | 1854 in two straight lines in centre. DUNSTABLE HOUSE in half circle above. CASHEL STREET | CHRISTCHURCH N.Z. in two half circular lines beneath.

No. 300. Penny. Size 21. Common.

Obv : EDWARD REECE | WHOLESALE | AND RETAIL | BUILDERS | AND FURNISHING | IRONMONGER | BIRMINGHAM | AND SHEFFIELD | WAREHOUSE | CHRISTCHURCH | CANTERBURY | N.Z. in twelve lines.

Rev: A wheatsheaf and sickle to left. A man seated on the ground shearing a sheep, to right. ADVANCE CANTERBURY in half circle above. NEW ZEALAND beneath.

No. 301. Halfpenny. Size 17½. Scarce.

Obv: and Rev: same as No. 300.

Dunedin.

No. 302. Penny. Size 21. Very common.

Obv: DAY & MIEVILLE | MERCHANTS | DUNEDIN | OTAGO displayed in four lines.

Rev: Same as No. 274.

No. 303. Penny. Size 19. Common.

Obv: Royal Arms (quarterly—1st and 4th three lions for England. 2nd, a lion rampant for Scotland. 3rd, a harp for Ireland) surrounded by the garter, on which is the motto—HONI SOIT QUI MAL Y PENSE the whole surmounted by a Crown. E. DE CARLE & CO MERCHANTS DUNEDIN OTAGO in old English letters around the arms.

Rev: Female seated on a bale, holding scales in right hand, and cornucopia in left, out of which is issuing fruits and flowers. Water and ship in the distance. VIVANT REGINA in half circle above. 1862 beneath.

No. 304. Penny. Size 21. Common.

Obv: JONES & WILLIAMSON | WHOLESALE | & | RETAIL | GROCERS, | WINE, SPIRIT, | & PROVISION | MERCHANTS | DUNEDIN displayed in nine lines.

Rev: Same as No. 268.

No. 305. Penny. Size 19. Scarce.

Obv: PERKINS & Co in half circle. DRAPERS in straight line in centre. DUNEDIN in half circle beneath.

Rev: Female seated on a bale, cask at back; scales in right hand, and horn of plenty in left, out of which is issuing fruits and flowers. Water and ship in the distance. DUNEDIN NEW ZEALAND in half circle above.

No. 306. Penny. Size 21. Scarce.

Obv: A. S. WILSON | DUNEDIN | OTAGO | MEDICAL HALL displayed in four lines.

Rev: Same as No. 274.

Grahamstown.

No. 307. Penny. Size 21. Scarce.

Obv: *George Mc Caul—Grahamstown*—COPPER-SMITH | TINSMITH | PLUMBER | AND | GASFITTER arranged in five lines in centre. 18 to left, 74 to right. The whole within an inner circle. Between the rim and the circle N · E · W · · · · Z · E · A · L · A · N · D · · · · extending all around the token.

Rev: Within a circle, a view of the shaft and engine house. ADVANCE | THAMES GOLDFIELDS at foot. Between the rim of the token and circle are 16 dots extending all round.

Invercargill.

No. 308. Size 19. Penny. Scarce.

Obv: S. BEAVEN | IRONMONGER | & | MERCHANT | INVERCARGILL N.Z. displayed in five lines.

Rev: Australian Arms. PEACE & PLENTY in half circle above. 1863 beneath.

This token is in the British Museum collection.

Nelson.

No. 309. Penny. Size 21. Common.

Obv: J. M. MERRINGTON & Co. | WHOLESALE | & | RETAIL | DRAPERS | & | OUTFITTERS | NELSON displayed in eight lines.

Rev: Female standing, holding scales in right hand and horn of plenty in left. ADVANCE NEW ZEALAND in half circle above.

New Plymouth.

No. 310. Penny. Size 19. Scarce.

Obv: JOHN GILMOUR in half circle. NEW | PLYMOUTH

in two lines in centre. NEW ZEALAND in half .circle beneath.

Rev :· In the foreground a Moa. Three palm trees to right. Water in the distance, on which is a canoe. A view of Mount Egmont in the back ground.

Taranaki.

No. 311. Penny. Size 19. Scarce.

Obv : BROWN AND DUTHIE | WHOLESALE | & RE- TAIL | IRONMONGERS | BROUGHAM STREET displayed in five lines.

Rev : A view of Mount Egmont. TARANAKI | 1866 in two lines beneath.

Timaru.

No. 312. Penny. Size 21. Scarce.

Obv : CLARKSON AND TURNBULL · 1865 · around the token between the dotted edge and dotted inner circle. GENERAL IMPORTERS | DRAPERS | CLOTHIERS | &c. in five straight lines within the circle in centre.

Rev : A view of Timaru harbour. Lighthouse at end of pier or breakwater. Steamship in harbour. NEW ZEALAND above. TIMARU beneath:

Wanganui.

No. 313. Penny. Size 19. Scarce.

Obv : J. HURLEY & Co. between two lines in centre. SHIPPING | SUPPLIED in two lines above. WANGANUI | NEW ZEALAND in two lines beneath the name; the whole within a dotted circle in centre. CONFECTIONERS, BAKERS, & GROCERS · ESTABLISHED 1853. around the token between the dotted edge and dotted inner circle.

Rev : Female seated. Anchor and two wheatsheaves to right. Bee hive, beneath which· is a cornucopia, out of which is issuing fruits and flowers. Bale and case to left. Water and ship in the distance. TODMAN LONDON in minute letters at foot of design.

No. 314. Halfpenny. Size 16. Scarce.

Obv: and Rev: Same as preceding, excepting that the comma is omitted after the word BAKERS on the obverse.

Wellington.

No. 315. Penny. Size 21. Common.

Obv: D. ANDERSON'S | GENERAL | STORES | · WELLINGTON · arranged in four lines.

Rev: Female facing left. Eyes bandaged. Scales in right hand, horn of plenty in left, out of which is issuing fruits and flowers. Water and ship in the distance. (Same as No. 215.)

No. 316. Halfpenny. Size 17½. Common.

Obv: and Rev: Same as preceding.

No. 317. Penny. Size 19. Scarce.

Obv: KIRKCALDIE & STAINS | GENERAL | DRAPERS | AND | OUTFITTERS | · WELLINGTON · displayed in six lines.

Rev: Arms and Crest, motto on scroll beneath (FORTISSIMA VERITAS). KIRKCALDIE & STAINS in half circle above. · WELLINGTON · beneath.

No. 318. Penny. Size 21. Common.

Obv: LIPMAN LEVY · | IMPORTER | AND | MANU-FACTURER | OF BOOTS | & SHOES | WELLINGTON. NEW ZEALAND displayed in seven lines.

Rev: ONE PENNY TOKEN. PAYABLE AT L. LEVY'S LAMBTON QUAY.—— around the token. LEATHER | & GRINDERY | OF ALL | DESCRIPTION | THE TRADE | SUPPLIED in six lines in centre.

No. 319. Penny. Size 21.

Obv: Same as No. 318.

Rev: Draped and laureated bust of Wellington to right. —WELLINGTON & ERIN GO BRAGH.

(Apparently a mule.)

No. 320. Penny. Size 21.

Obv: Same as No. 318.

Rev: Same as No. 75.—See note to No. 73 respecting this reverse.

This token is also in the finest condition, and apparently a mule.

No. 321. Halfpenny. Size 17½. Common.

Obv: and Rev: Same as No. 318, excepting that HALF-PENNY is substituted for PENNY on the reverse.

No. 322. Halfpenny. Size 17½.

Obv: and Rev: Same as No. 296 (a mule).

No. 323. Halfpenny. Size 17½. Common.

Obv: A saddle and stirrups in centre. ·J. W. MEARS· | SADDLER in two lines above. LAMBTON QUAY WELLING-TON in three parts of a circle beneath.

Rev: ONE HALFPENNY TOKEN | PAYABLE | AT | · J. W. MEARS | COLLAR & | HARNESS | MAKER | ·NEW ZEALAND · displayed in eight lines.

No. 324. Penny. Size 21. Common.

Obv: JAMES WALLACE in half circle above. GROCER | &c. in two straight lines in centre. ·WELLINGTON · in half circle beneath.

Rev: Same as No. 261.

No. 325. Halfpenny. Size 17½. Scarce.

Obv: and Rev: Same as preceding.

No. 321. O. Milner & Thompson's Canterbury Music Depot & Pianoforte Warehouse in circle. Sole Agents /for/ John Brinsmead /d Sons/ Pianos in 5 ll.

R. Bust of William with Spear & Shield. Ad arms New Zealand in ½ circle above.

(Counter marked on R. J. S.)

INDEX.

Brinsmead,
_3:6_

Breinigsville, PA USA
21 October 2010
247783BV00002B/18/P